Internet in an Hour 101 Things You Need to Know

Don Mayo

Acknowledgements

Thanks to Jen, Midori, and Monique: We did it!

Don Mayo

Managing Editor	Technical Editors	English Editor	Illustrations	Design and Layout
Jennifer Frew	Jennifer Frew Cathy Vesecky	Monique Peterson	Ryan Sather	Midori Nakamura Paul Wray Elsa Johannesson

ISBN: 1-56243-675-9
Cat. No. HR5
DDC Publishing, Inc. Printing:
10 9 8 7 6 5 4 3
Printed in the United States of America.

Contents

Contents

Introduction

This Book is Designed for You . . .

if you are new to the Internet and you need a simple answer to what seems a complex question. Or, maybe you just need the answer to a simple question, but you don't know who to ask. *Internet in an Hour: 101 Things You Need to Know* has the answers.

This book has two main sections, Internet Basics and 101 Things.

Internet Basics

In Internet Basics, you can learn how to:

- Use Netscape Navigator to browse the World Wide Web.
- Send and receive e-mail messages with Netscape Messenger.
- Use Internet Explorer to browse the World Wide Web.
- Send and receive e-mail messages with Microsoft Outlook Express.
- Access the Internet using America Online.
- Send and receive e-mail messages with America Online.
- Find information on the Web with search engines.

101 Things

101 Things shows you ways you can use the Internet more effectively. Organized around commonly used Internet functions, learn what you need to know in order to make the most of your time online. Each topic showcases the quickest and easiest ways to get things done.

What Do I Need to Use This Book?

This book assumes that you have some general knowledge and experience with computers and that you already know how to perform the following tasks:

- Use a mouse (double-click, etc.).
- Make your way around Microsoft Windows 95.
- Install and run programs.

If you are completely new to computers as well as the World Wide Web, you may want to refer to DDC's **Learning Microsoft Windows 95** or **Learning the Internet**.

This book also assumes that you have access to browser applications such as Microsoft Internet Explorer 4.0, Netscape Navigator 4.0, or America Online.

√ *If you do not currently have these applications, contact your Internet Service Provider for instructions on how to download them. You can also use other browsers or previous versions such as Explorer 3.0 and Navigator 3.0 to browse the Web.*

You must have an Internet connection, either through your school, your office, or an online service such as America Online or CompuServe. How to get connected to the Internet is not covered in this book.

Please read over the following list of "must haves" to ensure that you are ready to be connected to the Internet.

- A computer (with a recommended minimum of 16 MB of RAM) and a modem port.
- A modem (with a recommended minimum speed of 14.4kbps, and suggested speed of 28.8kbps) that is connected to an analog phone line (assuming you are not using a direct Internet connection through a school, corporation, etc.).
- Established access to the Internet through an online service, independent Internet service provider, etc.
- A great deal of patience. The Internet is a fun and exciting place. But getting connected can be frustrating at times. Expect to run into occasional glitches, to get disconnected from time to time, and to experience occasional difficulty in viewing certain Web pages or features. The more up-to-date your equipment and software are, however, the less difficulty you will probably experience.

Internet Cautions

ACCURACY:

Be cautious not to believe everything on the Internet. Almost anyone can publish information on the Internet, and since there is no Internet editor or monitor, some information may be false. All information found on the World Wide Web should be checked for accuracy through additional reputable sources.

SECURITY:

When sending information over the Internet, be prepared to let the world have access to it. Computer hackers can find ways to access anything that you send to anyone over the Internet, including e-mail. Be cautious when sending confidential information to anyone.

VIRUSES:

These small, usually destructive computer programs hide inside of innocent-looking programs. Once a virus is executed, it attaches itself to other programs. When triggered, often by the occurrence of a date or time on the computer's internal clock/calendar, it executes a nuisance or damaging function, such as displaying a message on your screen, corrupting your files, or reformatting your hard disk.

B
A
S
I
C
S

Netscape Navigator: 1

◆ **About Netscape Navigator** ◆ **Start Netscape Navigator**
◆ **The Netscape Screen** ◆ **Exit Netscape Navigator**

About Netscape Navigator

■ Netscape Navigator 4.0 is the Internet browser component of
Netscape Communicator, a set of integrated tools for browsing the
World Wide Web, finding and downloading information, shopping for
and purchasing goods and services, creating Web pages, and
communicating with others with e-mail. This chapter focuses on the
Netscape Navigator browser. Netscape Messenger, the e-mail
component, is covered in Chapters 4-6.

Start Netscape Navigator

To start Netscape Navigator (Windows 95):

• Click the Start button ⊞ Start .

• Click Programs, Netscape Communicator, Netscape Navigator.

OR

• If you have a shortcut to Netscape Communicator ⊞ on your
desktop, double-click it to start Netscape Navigator.

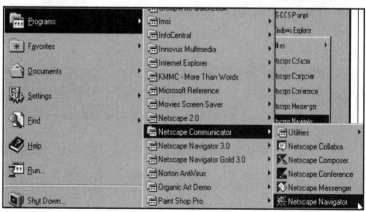

√ *The first time you start Netscape Communicator, the New Profile Setup dialog
box appears. Enter information about your e-mail name and service provider in
the dialog boxes that appear. If you do not know the information, you can leave
it blank until you are ready to fill it in.*

2

The Netscape Screen

■ The Netscape Navigator screen contains features that will be very helpful as you explore the Internet. Some of these features are constant and some change depending on the Web site visited or the task attempted or completed.

√ *To gain more space on screen, you may want to hide toolbars and the Location line. Go to the View menu and select the desired hide/show options.*

Title bar   Displays the name of the program (Netscape) and the current Web page (Welcome to Netscape). Note the standard Windows minimize, maximize/restore, and close buttons at the right.

Menu bar   Displays menus, which provide drop-down lists of commands for executing Netscape tasks.

Navigation toolbar   Contains buttons for moving between and printing Web pages. The name and icon on each button identify the command for the button. You can access these commands quickly and easily by clicking the mouse on the desired button.

If the toolbar buttons are not visible, open the View menu and click Show Navigation Toolbar.

Location toolbar   Displays the electronic address of the currently displayed Web page in the Location field. You can also type the electronic address of a Web page in the Location field and press Enter to access it. A Web site address is called a Uniform Resource Locator (URL).

If the Location toolbar is not visible, open the View menu and click Show Location Toolbar.

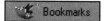 The Location toolbar also contains the Bookmarks QuickFile button. Click this button to view a list of sites that you have bookmarked for quick access. (For more information on bookmarks, see "Netscape Navigator: 3" on page 9.)

 The Location button is also located on this toolbar. The word *Netsite* displays if the current Web site uses Netscape software. The word *Location* replaces Netsite if the site does not use Netscape as its primary software.

Personal toolbar
Contains buttons or links that you add to connect to your favorite sites. When you install Netscape Communicator, the Internet, Lookup, New&Cool, and Netcaster buttons are on the Personal toolbar by default. You can delete these buttons and add your own by displaying the desired Web site and dragging the Location icon onto the Personal toolbar.

Netscape's status indicator
Netscape's icon  pulses when Netscape is processing a request (command) that you enter. To return immediately to Netscape's home page, click on this icon.

Status bar
When a Web page is opening, the Status bar indicates progress by a percentage displayed in the center and the security level of the page being loaded by a lock in the far-left corner. When you place the cursor over a hyperlink, the Status bar displays the URL of the link.

Component toolbar
The buttons on this toolbar are links to other Communicator components: Navigator, (Messenger) Mailbox, (Collabra) Discussions, and (Page) Composer.

Exit Netscape Navigator

- Exiting Netscape Navigator and disconnecting from your Internet Service Provider (ISP) are two separate steps. You can actually disconnect from your service provider and still have Netscape Navigator open. (Remember that you must first establish a connection to the Internet via your ISP to use Netscape to access information on the Web.) You can also disconnect from Navigator and still have your ISP open.

- There are times when you may want to keep Netscape open to read information obtained from the Web, access information stored on your hard disk using Netscape, or to compose e-mail to send later. If you don't disconnect from your ISP and you pay an hourly rate, you will continue incurring charges.

CAUTION   When you exit Netscape, you do not necessarily exit from your Internet service provider. Be sure to check the disconnect procedure from your ISP so that you will not continue to be charged for time online. Most services disconnect when a certain amount of time passes with no activity.

√   *Once you disconnect from your ISP, you can no longer access new Web information. Remember: Netscape Navigator is a browser; it is not an Internet connection.*

√   *You can disconnect from your ISP and view Web information accessed during the current session using the Back and Forward toolbar buttons. This is because the visited sites are stored in the memory of your computer. However, Web sites visited during the current session are erased from your computer memory when you exit Netscape.*

Netscape Navigator: 2

◆ **The Navigation Toolbar**
◆ **URLs (Uniform Resource Locator)** ◆ **Open World Wide Web Sites**

The Navigation Toolbar

- The Netscape Navigation toolbar displays buttons for Netscape's most commonly used commands. Note that each button contains an icon and a word describing the button's function. Choosing any of these buttons activates the indicated task immediately.

- If the Navigation toolbar is not visible, select Show Navigation Toolbar from the View menu.

 Moves back through pages previously displayed. Back is available only if you have moved around among Web pages in the current Navigator session; otherwise, it is dimmed.

 Moves forward through pages previously displayed. Forward is available only if you have used the Back button; otherwise, it is dimmed.

 Reloads the currently displayed Web page. Use this button if the current page is taking too long to display or to update the current page with any changes that may have been made since the page was downloaded.

 Displays the home page.

 Displays Netscape's Net Search Page. You can select one of several search tools from this page.

 Displays a menu with helpful links to Internet sites that contain search tools and services.

 Prints the displayed page, topic, or article.

 Displays security information for the displayed Web page as well as information on Netscape security features.

Stops the loading of a Web page.

URLs (Uniform Resource Locator)

- Every Web site has a unique address called its URL (Uniform Resource Locator). A URL has four parts:

Part	Example	Description
Protocol	**http://**	The protocol indicates the method used for communicating on the internet The most common is http:// , which stands for Hypertext Transfer Protocol. Another protocol—ftp:// (file transfer protocol)—is used with internet sites designed to make files available for uploading and downloading.
Address type	**www.**	www. stands for World Wide Web and indicates that the site is located on the Web. Occasionally, you may find other address types, but www. addresses are the most common.
Identifier of the site's owner	**ddcpub**	This part of the address identifies who is responsible for the Web site.
Domain	**.com, .gov, .org, .edu, etc.** (see below)	The domain indicates the kind of organization that sponsors the site (company, government, non-profit organization, educational institution, and so on).

- For example, the DDC publishing URL breaks down as follows:

http://www.ddcpub.com

Hypertext Transfer Protocol   World Wide Web   Company name   Domain

- There are seven common domains:

com	Commercial enterprise	**edu**	Educational institution
org	Non-commercial organization	**mil**	U. S. Military location
net	A network that has a gateway to the Internet	**gov**	Local, state, or federal government location
int	International organization		

Open World Wide Web Sites

- There are several ways to access a Web site. If you know the site's address, you can enter the correct Web address (URL) on the Location field on the Location toolbar.

- If the address you are entering is the address of a site you have visited recently or that you have bookmarked (see "Netscape Navigator: 3" on page 9 for more information on Bookmarks), you will notice as you begin to type the address that Netscape attempts to complete it for you. If the address that Netscape suggests is the one you want, press Enter.

- If the address that Netscape suggests is not correct, keep typing to complete the desired address and then press Enter. Or, you can click the down arrow next to the Location field to view a list of other possible matches, select an address, and press Enter.

- You can also enter the URL in the Open Page dialog box. To do so, select Open Page from the File menu, select Navigator, type the URL, and click Open.

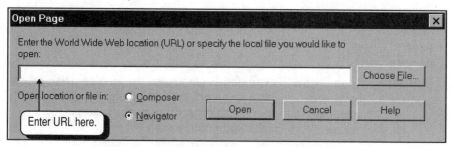

- There are a couple of shortcuts for entering URL addresses. One shortcut involves omitting the http://www. prefix from the Web address. Netscape assumes the **http://** protocol and the **www** that indicates that the site is located on the Web. If you are trying to connect to a company Web site, entering the company name is generally sufficient. Netscape assumes the **.com** suffix. For example, entering **ddcpub** on the location line and pressing Enter would reach the **http://www.ddcpub.com** address.

√ *Don't be discouraged if the connection to the World Wide Web site is not made immediately. The site may be off-line temporarily. The site may also be very busy with others users trying to access it. Be sure the URL is typed accurately. Occasionally, it takes several tries to connect to a site.*

Netscape Navigator: 3

◆ History List ◆ Bookmarks ◆ Add Bookmarks
◆ Delete Bookmarks ◆ Print Web Pages

History List

- While you move back and forth among Web sites, Netscape automatically records each of these site locations in a **history** list, which is temporarily stored on your computer. You can use the history list to track what sites you have already visited or to jump to a recently viewed site.

  √ *As you move from one site to another on the Web, you may find yourself asking, "How did I get here?" The History list is an easy way to see the path you followed to get to the current destination.*

- To view the history list, click <u>H</u>istory on the <u>C</u>ommunicator menu, or press Ctrl+H. To link to a site shown in the history list, double-click on it.

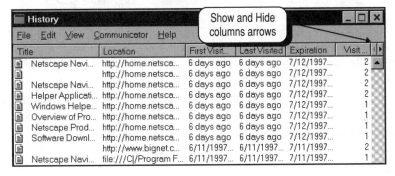

Bookmarks

- A **bookmark** is a placeholder containing the title and URL of a Web page that, when selected, links directly to that page. If you find a Web site that you like and want to revisit, you can create a bookmark to record its location. (See "Add Bookmarks" on page 10.) The Netscape bookmark feature maintains permanent records of the Web sites in your bookmark files so that you can return to them easily.

- You can view the Bookmarks menu by selecting <u>B</u>ookmarks from the <u>C</u>ommunicator menu or by clicking on the Bookmarks QuickFile button 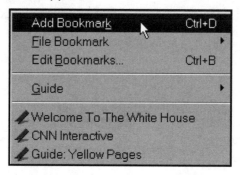 on the Location toolbar. The drop-down menu shown below appears.

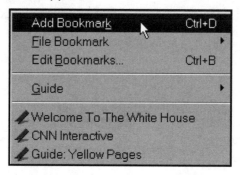

Add Bookmarks

- Display the Web page to add, go to <u>B</u>ookmarks on the <u>C</u>ommunicator menu and click Add Bookmar<u>k</u>.

Netscape does not confirm that a bookmark has been added to the file.

- You can create bookmarks from addresses in the History folder. Click <u>C</u>ommunicator, <u>H</u>istory and select the listing to bookmark. Right-click on it and choose Add To Bookmar<u>k</u>s from the menu.

Delete Bookmarks

- Bookmarks may be deleted at anytime. For example, you may wish to delete a bookmark if a Web site no longer exists or remove one that is no longer of interest to you.
- To delete a bookmark do the following:
  - Click <u>C</u>ommunicator.
  - Click <u>B</u>ookmarks.
  - Click Edit <u>B</u>ookmarks.
  - In the Bookmarks window, select the bookmark you want to delete by clicking on it from the bookmark list.
  - Press the Delete key.

10

OR

- Right-click on the bookmark and select <u>D</u>elete Bookmark from the drop-down menu.

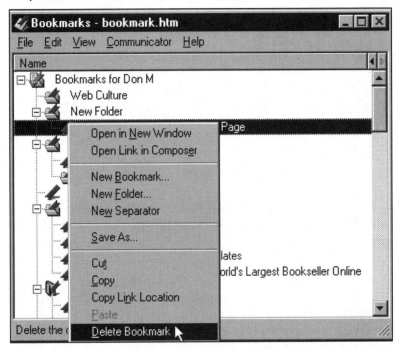

Print Web Pages

- One of the many uses of the Internet is to print out information. You can print a page as it appears on screen, or you can print it as plain text. Only displayed pages can be printed.

- To print a Web page, display it and do the following:

  - Click the Print button [Print] on the Navigation toolbar.

  OR

  - Click <u>P</u>rint on the <u>F</u>ile menu.

  - In the Print dialog box that displays, select the desired print options and click Print.

- In most cases, the Web page will be printed in the format shown in the Web page display.

Netscape Messenger: 4

Configure Netscape Mail

√   *This section assumes that you have already set up an e-mail account with a service provider. If you do not have an e-mail address, contact your Internet Service Provider. Establishing a modem connection and configuring your computer to send and receive mail can be frustrating. Don't be discouraged; what follows are steps that will get you connected, but some of the information may have to be supplied by your Internet Service Provider. Calling for help will save you time and frustration.*

■ The Netscape Communicator browser suite includes a comprehensive e-mail program called Netscape Messenger, which allows you to send, receive, save, and print e-mail messages and attachments.

■ Before you can use Messenger to send and receive e-mail, you must configure the program with your e-mail account information (user name, e-mail address, and mail server names). You may have already filled in this information if you completed the New Profile Setup Wizard when you installed Netscape Communicator.

■ You may have configured Netscape Messenger to receive and send e-mail messages when you first installed the program. If not, follow these steps to get connected. You can also use these steps to update and change settings to your e-mail account.

Identity Settings

• Open the Edit menu on the Netscape Navigator or Netscape Messenger menu and select Preferences. Click Identity in the Mail & Groups Category list to and do the following:

Enter your name and e-mail address in the first two boxes. Enter any other optional information in the Identity dialog box.

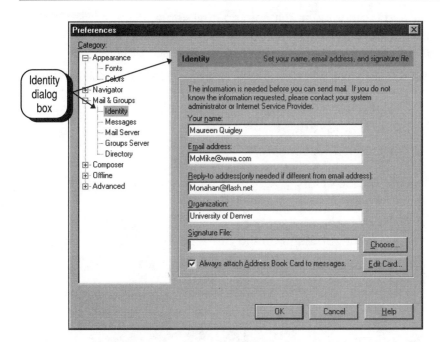

Mail Server Preference Settings

- Click Mail Server to configure your mailbox so that you can send and receive mail.

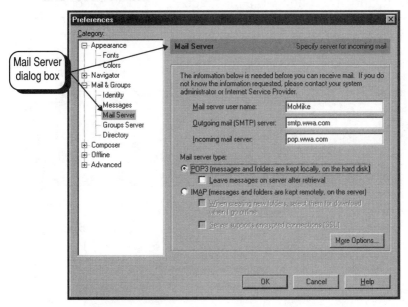

- Enter mail server user name in the first box. This is usually the part of your e-mail address that appears in front of the @ sign.

- Enter your outgoing and incoming mail server. Check with your Internet Service Provider if you are not sure what these settings are.

- Click OK to save and close the Preference settings. You should now be able to send and receive e-mail messages and/or files.

Start Netscape Messenger

■ To start Netscape Messenger:

- Click the Mailbox icon  on the Component bar.

  OR

- Start the Netscape Messenger program from the Netscape Communicator submenu on the Start menu.

KMMC - More Than Words ▶	Netscape Collabra
Microsoft Reference ▶	Netscape Composer
Movies Screen Saver ▶	Netscape Conference
Netscape 2.0 ▶	Netscape Messenger
Netscape Communicator ▶	Netscape Navigator

The Message List Window

■ After you launch Messenger, a message list window will open, displaying the contents of the e-mail Inbox folder. You can retrieve, read, forward, and reply to messages from this window.

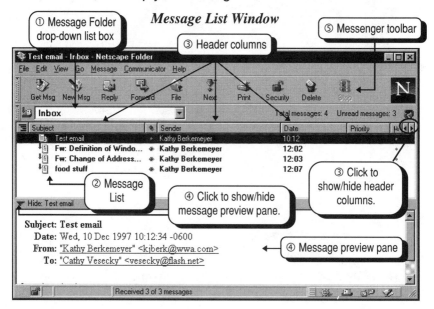

Message List Window

- The message list window includes the following:

① The **Message Folder drop-down list box** displays the currently selected message folder, the contents of which are displayed in the message list below the drop-down box. Click the down arrow to display a list of other message folders. Select a different folder from the list to display its contents in the message list area.

② The **message list** displays a header for each of the messages contained in the currently selected message folder (Inbox is the default).

③ **Header columns** list the categories of information available for each message, such as subject, sender, and date. You can customize the display of the header columns in a number of ways:

  - Resize column widths by placing the mouse pointer over the right border of a column until the pointer changes to a double arrow, and then click and drag the border to the desired size.

  - Rearrange the order of the columns by clicking and dragging a header to a new location in the series.

  - Show/hide different columns by clicking the arrow buttons on the upper-right side of the message list window.

    √ *If text in a message header is cut off so that you cannot read it all, position the mouse pointer on the header in the column containing the cropped text. A small box will display the complete text for that column of the header, as in the example below:*

④ The **message preview pane** displays the content of the message currently selected from the message list. You can show/hide the preview pane by clicking on the blue triangle icon in the bottom-left corner of the message list pane. You can resize the preview pane or the message list pane by placing the pointer over the border between the two panes until the pointer changes to a double arrow and then dragging the border up or down to the desired size.

⑤ The **Messenger toolbar** displays buttons for activating Netscape Messenger's most commonly used commands. Note that each button contains an image and a word describing the function. Choosing any of these buttons will activate the indicated task immediately.

Messenger Toolbar Buttons and Functions

 Retrieves new mail from your Internet mail server and loads it into the Inbox message folder.

 Opens the Message Composition screen allowing you to compose new mail messages.

 Allows you to reply to the sender of an e-mail message or to the sender and all other recipients of the e-mail message.

 Forwards a message you have received to another address.

 Stores the current message in one of six Messenger default file folders or in a new folder that you create.

 Selects and displays the next of the unread messages in your Inbox.

 Prints the displayed message.

 Displays the security status of a message.

 Deletes the selected message. Deleted messages are moved to the Trash folder. You must delete contents of Trash folder to remove messages from your computer.

Get New Mail

- Since new e-mail messages are stored on a remote ISP mail server, you must be connected to the Internet to access them. To retrieve new messages to your computer, click the Get Msg button on the Messenger toolbar.

- In the Password Entry dialog box that follows, enter your e-mail password in the blank text box and click OK. (If you do not know your e-mail password, contact your ISP.)

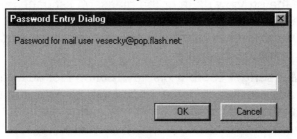

√ *Messenger saves your password for the rest of the current Messenger session. You must re-enter it each time you retrieve new mail, unless you set Messenger to save your password permanently. To do so:*

- Click Edit, Preferences.
- Click once on Mail Server under Mail & Groups.
- Click the More Options button.
- Select the Remember my mail password check box and click OK twice.

■ The Getting New Messages box opens, displaying the status of your message retrieval.

■ Once your new messages are retrieved, they are listed in the message list window. By default, Messenger stores new mail messages in the Inbox folder.

Read Messages

■ You can read a message in the preview pane of the message list window or in a separate window.

■ To read a message in the preview pane, click on the desired message header in the message list. If the message does not appear, click on the blue triangle icon at the bottom of the message list window to display the preview pane.

■ To open and read a message in a separate window, double-click on the desired message header in the message list. You can close a message after reading it by clicking File, Close or by clicking on the Close button (X) in the upper-right corner of the window.

■ To read the next unread message, click the Next button [Next] on the Messenger toolbar. Or, if you have reached the end of the current message, you can press the spacebar to proceed to the next unread message.

- Once you have read a message, it remains stored in the Inbox folder until you delete it or file it in another folder. (See "Delete a Message" below.)

  √ *You do not have to be online to read e-mail. You can reduce your online charges if you disconnect from your ISP after retrieving your messages and read them offline.*

  √ *Icons located to the left of message headers in the message list identify each message as either unread* ▣ *(retrieved during a previous Messenger session), new* ▣ *(and unread), or read* ▣.

Delete a Message

- To delete a message, select its header from the message list window and click the Delete button | Delete | in the Messenger toolbar.

  √ *To select more than one message to delete, click the Ctrl button while you click each message header.*

Print Messages

- In order to print a message you must first display the message in either the preview pane of the message list window or in a separate window, then:

  • Click the Print button | Print | on the Messenger toolbar.

  • In the Print dialog box that appears, select the desired print options and click OK.

Print Dialog Box

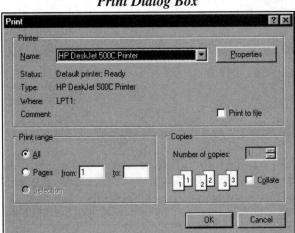

Bookmark a Message

- You can add an e-mail message to your Bookmarks folder for easy access from anywhere within the Communicator suite. To bookmark a message:

  - Display the message you want to bookmark in either the preview pane of the message list window or in a separate window.

  - Select Communicator, Bookmarks, Add Bookmark.

- Messenger will add the message to the bottom of your Bookmarks menu.

Netscape Messenger: 5

◆ Compose New Messages ◆ Send Messages
◆ The Message Composition Toolbar ◆ Reply to Mail
◆ Forward Mail ◆ Add Entries to the Personal Address Book
◆ Address a New Message Using the Personal Address Book

Compose New Messages

■ You can compose an e-mail message in Netscape Messenger while you are connected to the Internet, or while you are offline. When composing an e-mail message online, you can send the message immediately after creating it. When composing a message offline (which is considered proper Netiquette—net etiquette), you will need to store the message in your Unsent Messages folder until you are online and can send it.

■ To create a message, you first need to open Messenger's Message Composition window. To do so:

• Click the New Message button New Msg .

√ *The Message Composition window displays.*

Netscape Message Composition Window

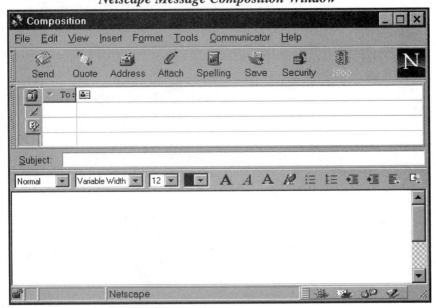

√ *You can hide any toolbar in the Message Composition screen by going to View, Hide Message Toolbar or Hide Formatting Toolbar.*

√ *If you do not know the recipient's address, you can look it up and insert it from your personal address book (see page 24) or an online directory.*

■ In the Message Composition window, type the Internet address(es) of the message recipient(s) in the To: field. Or, click the Address button [Address] on the Message Composition toolbar and select an address to insert (see pages 24-26 for more information on using the Address Book).

√ *If you are sending the message to multiple recipients, press Enter after typing each recipient's address.*

■ After inserting the address(es), click the To: icon [▾ To:] to display a drop-down menu of other addressee options. Select any of the following options from the drop-down menu and enter the recipient information indicated.

To	The e-mail address of the person to whom the message is being sent.
CC (Carbon Copy)	The e-mail addresses of people who will receive copies of the message.
BCC (Blind Carbon Copy)	Same as CC, except these names will not appear anywhere in the message, so other recipients will not know that the person(s) listed in the BCC field received a copy.
Group	Names of newsgroups that will receive this message (similar to Mail To).
Reply To	The e-mail address where replies should be sent.
Follow-up To	Another newsgroup heading; used to identify newsgroups to which comments should be posted (similar to Reply To).

■ Click in the Subject field (or press Tab to move the cursor there) and type the subject of the message.

■ Click in the blank composition area below the Subject field and type the body of your message. Word wrap occurs automatically, and you can cut and paste quotes from other messages or text from other programs. You can also check the spelling of your message by clicking on the Spelling button 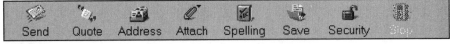 on the Message Composition toolbar and responding to the dialog prompts that follow.

Send Messages

- Once you have created a message, you have three choices:
  - to send the message immediately
  - to store the message in the Unsent Messages folder to be sent later (File, Send Later)
  - to save the message in the Drafts folder to be finished and sent later (File, Save Draft)

To send a message immediately:

- Click the Send button Send on the Message Composition toolbar.

The Message Composition Toolbar

- The toolbar in the Message Composition window has several features that are specific only to this screen.
- Notice that the main toolbar buttons contain a task name and illustration.

Message Composition Toolbar

	Immediately sends current message.
	Used when replying to a message, the Quote feature allows you to include text from the original message.
	Select an address from the addresses stored in your personal address book to insert into address fields.
	By clicking the Attach button, you can send a file, a Web page, or your personal address card along with your e-mail message.
	Checks for spelling errors in the current message.

Lets you save your message as a draft for later use.

 Sets the security status of a message.

 Stops the display of an HTML message or a message with an HTML attachment.

- The Formatting toolbar provides commands for applying styles, fonts, font size, bulleted lists, and inserting objects.

Reply to Mail

- To reply to a message, select or open the message to reply to and click the Reply button 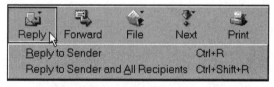.

- From the submenu that appears, select Reply to Sender to reply to the original sender only, or select Reply to Sender and All Recipients to send a reply to the sender and all other recipients of the original message. Selecting one of these options lets you reply to the message without having to enter the recipient's name or e-mail address.

√ *The Message Composition window opens, with the To, Cc, and Subject fields filled in for you.*

- Compose your reply as you would a new message.

- To include a copy of the original message with your reply, click the Quote button on the Message Composition toolbar. You can edit the original message and header text as you wish.

- When you are finished, click the Send button to send the message immediately.

Forward Mail

- To forward a message automatically without having to enter the recipient's name or e-mail address, first select or open the message to forward. Then click on the Forward button .

  The Message Composition window opens, with the Subject field filled in for you.

Subject:	[Fwd: Andy's Birthday Party]

- Type the e-mail address of the new recipient in the To field, or click the Address button ⌨ Address on the Message Composition toolbar and select a name from your Address Book (see "Address a New Message Using the Personal Address Book" on page 26 for information on using the Address Book).

- If the original message does not appear in the composition area, click the Quote button 🖋 Quote on the Message Composition toolbar to insert it.

- Click in the composition area and edit the message as desired. You can also type any additional text you want to include with the forwarded message.

- When you are done, click the Send button 📁 Send to send the message immediately. Or, select Send Later from the File menu to store the message in the Unsent Messages mailbox to be sent later. To save the reply as a draft to be edited and sent later, select Save Draft from the File menu.

Add Entries to the Personal Address Book

- You can compile a personal address book to store e-mail addresses and other information about your most common e-mail recipients. You can then use the address book to find and automatically insert an address when creating a new message.

- To add a name to the address book:

  - Select Address Book from the Communicator menu. The Address Book window displays.

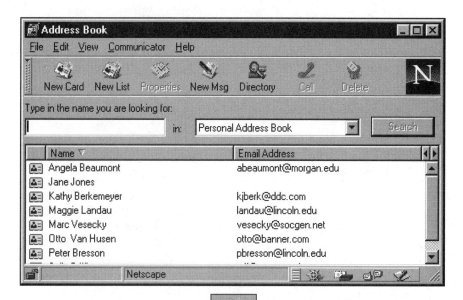

- Click the New Card button 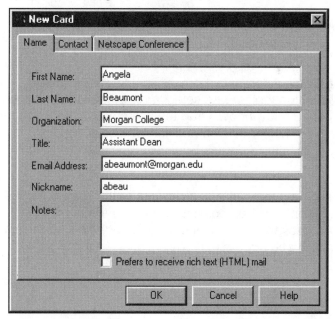 on the Address Book toolbar.
- In the New Card box that appears, enter the recipient's first name, last name, organization, title, and e-mail address.

- In the Nickname field, type a nickname for the recipient, if desired (the nickname must be unique among the entries in your address book). When addressing a message, you can use the recipient's nickname in the To field, rather than typing the entire address, and Messenger will automatically fill in the full e-mail address.

- In the Notes field, type any notes you want to store about the recipient.
- Click the Contact tab, if desired, and enter the recipient's postal address and phone number.
- Click OK.

■ You can edit an address book entry at any time by double-clicking on the person's name in the Address Book window.

■ You can automatically add the name and address of the sender of a message you are reading by selecting Add to Address Book from the Message menu and selecting Sender from the submenu. The New Card dialog box opens, with the First Name, Last Name, and E-mail Address fields filled in for you. You can enter a nickname for the person, if desired, and any other information you want in the remaining fields.

Address a New Message Using the Personal Address Book

■ To insert an address from your address book into a new message:

- Click the New Msg button to open the Message Composition window.

- Click on the Address button on the Message Composition toolbar and select a recipient(s) from the list in the Address Book window. Drag the selected name(s) into the To field in the Message Composition window. Click the Close button ⊠ in the Address Book window when you are finished.

  OR

- Begin typing the name or nickname of the recipient in the To field of the Message Composition window. If the name is included in the Address Book, Messenger will recognize it and finish entering the name and address for you.

◆ Attached Files ◆ View File Attachments
◆ Save Attached Files ◆ Attach Files to Messages

Attached Files

■ Sometimes an e-mail message will come with a separate file(s) attached. Messages containing attachments are indicated when you display a message and it contains a paperclip icon to the right of the message header. Attachment can be used, for example, when you want to send someone an Excel spreadsheet or a video clip.

■ With Messenger, you can view both plain text attachments and binary attachments. **Binary** files are files containing more than plain text (i.e., images, sound clips, and formatted text, such as spreadsheets and word processor documents).

■ Almost any e-mail program can read plain text files. Binary files, however, must be decoded by the receiving e-mail program before they can be displayed in readable form. This requires that the e-mail software have the capability to decode either MIME (Multi-Purpose Internet Mail Extension) or UUEncode protocol. Messenger can decode both. When a binary attachment arrives, Messenger automatically recognizes and decodes it.

View File Attachments

■ File or HTML attachments are displayed in one of two ways.

  • If you select View, Attachments, Inline, you see the attachment appended to the body of the message in a separate attachment window below the message. Essentially there is a series of sequential windows—one with the message and the other with the attachment.

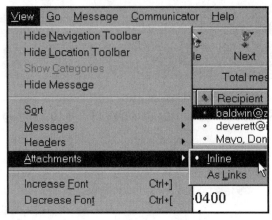

√ *Only plain text, images, and Web page attachments can be viewed inline.*

- If the attachment is HTML code, you will see a fully formatted Web page.

- If you select <u>V</u>iew, Attachments, As <u>L</u>inks, the attachment window displays an attachment box displaying the details of the attachment. It also serves as a link to the attachment.

√ *Viewing attachments as links reduces the time it takes to open a message on screen.*

- Clicking on the blue-highlighted text in the attachment box will display the attachment.

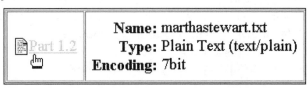

- You can right-click on the attachment icon box to display a menu of mail options such as forwarding, replying, or deleting the message.

  - By right-clicking on the actual attachment, you can choose from several file save options, such as saving the image or file in a separate file on your hard drive, as Windows wallpaper, or saving the image and putting a shortcut to the image on your desktop.

  - If you open a Web page attachment while online, you will find that the Web page serves as an actual connection to the Web site and that all links on the page are active. If you are not connected, the Web page will display fully formatted, but it will not be active.

- If an attached image displays as a link even after you select <u>V</u>iew, Attachments, <u>I</u>nline, it is probably because it is an image type that Messenger does not recognize. In this case, you need to install and/or open a plug-in or program with which to view the unrecognized image.

■ If you know you have the appropriate application or plug-in installed, click the Save File button in the Unknown File Type dialog box and save the attachment to your hard drive or disk (see "Save Attached Files" below). Then start the necessary application or plug-in and open the saved attachment file to view it.

■ If you do not have the necessary application or plug-in, click on the More Info button in the Unknown File Type dialog box. The Netscape Plug-in Finder Web page opens, displaying some general information about plug-ins, a list of plug-ins that will open the selected attachment, and hyperlinks to Web sites where you can download the given plug-ins.

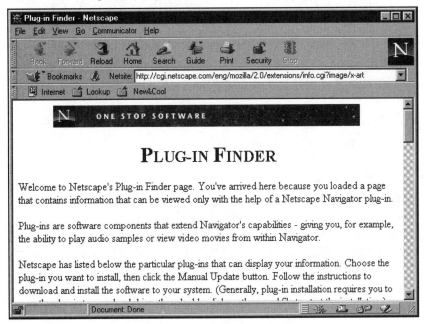

Save Attached Files

■ You can save an attached file to your hard drive or disk for future use or reference. To save an attachment:

• Open the message containing the attachment to save.

• If the attachment is in inline view, convert it to a link (View, Attachments, As Links).

• Right-click on the link and select Save Link As.

OR

- Click on the link to open the attachment. Select File, Save As, or, if Messenger does not recognize the attachment's file type, click the Save File button in the Unknown File Type dialog box.

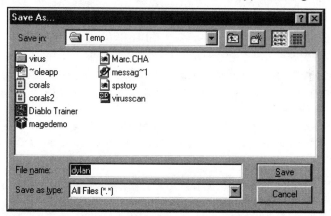

- In the Save As dialog box that follows, click the Save in drop-down list box and select the drive and folder(s) in which to save the file.

- Click in the File name text box and type a name for the file.

- Click Save.

Attach Files to Messages

- With Messenger, you can attach both plain text and binary files (images, media clips, formatted text documents, etc.) to e-mail messages. You may wish to check if your recipient's e-mail software can decode MIME or UUEncode protocols. Otherwise, binary attachments will not open and display properly on the recipient's computer.

- To attach a file to an e-mail message:

- Click the Attach button ⌸ on the Message Composition toolbar, and select File from the drop-down menu that appears.

- In the Enter file to attach dialog box that follows, click the Look in drop-down list box and select the drive and folder containing the file to attach.

- Then select the file to attach and click Open.

30

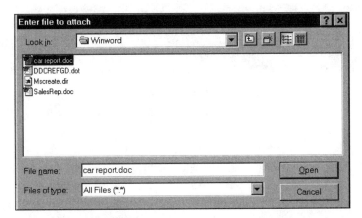

- After you have attached a file, the Attachments field in the Mail Composition window displays the name and location of the attached file.

  √ *Messages containing attachments usually take longer to send than those without attachments. When attaching very large files or multiple files, you may want to zip (compress) the files before attaching them. To do so, both you and the recipient need a file compression program, such as WinZip or PKZip.*

Attach Files and Documents

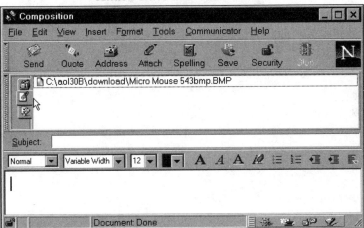

- Once you have attached the desired files and finished composing your message, you can send the e-mail, save it in the Unsent Messages folder for later delivery, or save it as a draft for later editing.

◆ **Start Internet Explorer 4**
◆ **Internet Explorer Screen** ◆ **Exit Internet Explorer**

Start Internet Explorer 4

- When you first install Internet Explorer and you are using the Active Desktop, you may see the message illustrated below when you turn on your computer. If you are familiar with Explorer 3, you may want to select 1 Take a Quick Tour to learn the new features in Explorer 4. Select 2 to learn about Channels.

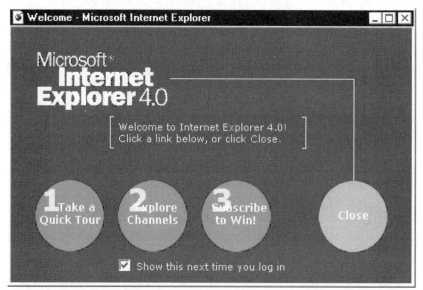

- To start Internet Explorer, do one of the following:

  - Click 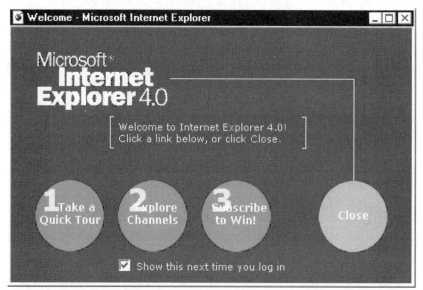 on the Desktop.

    OR

  - Click on the taskbar.

    OR

  - Click the Start button , then select Programs, Internet Explorer, and click Internet Explorer.

Internet Explorer Screen

- When you connect to the World Wide Web, the first screen that displays is called a home page. The term home page can be misleading since the first page of *any* World Wide Web site is called a home page. This first page is also sometimes referred to as the start page. You could think of the home/start page as the starting point of your trip on the information highway. Just as you can get on a highway using any number of on ramps, you can get on the Internet at different starting points.

- You can change the first page that you see when you connect to the Internet. To do this select View, Internet Options, then enter a new address in the Address text box.

  √ The page that you see when you are connected may differ from the one illustrated below.

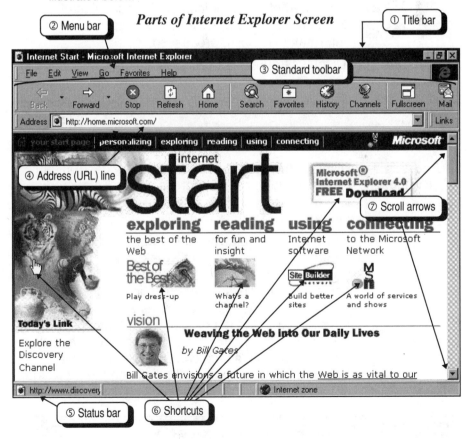

Parts of Internet Explorer Screen

① **Title bar**   Displays the name of the program and the current Web page. You can minimize, restore, or close Explorer using the buttons on the right side of the Title bar.

② **Menu bar**   Displays menus currently available, which provide drop-down lists of commands for executing Internet Explorer tasks.

     The Internet Explorer icon on the right side of the Menu bar rotates when action is occurring or information is being processed.

③ **Standard toolbar**   Displays frequently used commands.

④ **Address (URL) line**   Displays the address of the current page. You can click here, type a new address, press Enter, and go to a new location (if it's an active Web site). You can also start a search from this line.

If you click on the arrow at the right end of the address line, you will see the links that you have visited during the current Internet session. The Links bar, containing links to various Microsoft sites is concealed on the right side of the address bar. Drag the split bar to the left or somewhere else on the screen to display current Links. If you double-click the Links button, all the current links will display. Double-click again to hide the links on the right side of the menu bar. You can add/delete links.

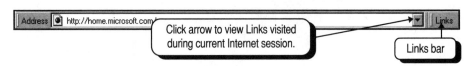

Note in the illustration above that the Links button has moved to the left side of the address bar. Just double-click on the Links button again to restore the address line. You can also drag the move bar, next to the Links button, to the left so that the Links and the Address line will both display. Drag the Links button down to display the contents of the Links bar directly below the Address bar (see illustration below).

⑤ **Status bar**   Displays information about actions occurring on the page and the Security Level. Internet Security Properties lets you control content that is downloaded on to your computer.

⑥ **Shortcuts**   Click on shortcuts (also called hyperlinks) to move to other Web sites. Shortcuts are usually easy to recognize. They can be underlined text, text of different colors, "buttons" of various sizes and shapes, or graphics. An easy way to tell if you are pointing to a shortcut is by watching the mouse pointer as it moves over the page. When it changes to a hand, you are on a shortcut. When you point to a shortcut the full name of the Web site will appear on the Status bar.

⑦ **Scroll arrows**   Scroll arrows are used to move the screen view, as in all Windows applications.

Exit Internet Explorer

- Exiting Internet Explorer and disconnecting from your service provider are two separate steps. It is important to remember that if you close Internet Explorer (or any other browser), you must also disconnect (or hang up) from your service provider. If you don't disconnect, you'll continue incurring charges.

CAUTION *When you exit Internet Explorer, you do not necessarily exit from your Internet service provider. Be sure to check the disconnect procedure from your ISP so that you will not continue to be charged for time online. Some services automatically disconnect when a specific amount of time has passed with no activity.*

Microsoft Internet Explorer: 8

◆ **Standard Toolbar Buttons**
◆ **Open a World Wide Web Site from the Address Bar**
◆ **Open a World Wide Web Site Using the File Open Dialog Box**

Internet Explorer Toolbar

Standard Toolbar Buttons

- The **Internet Explorer Standard toolbar** displays frequently used commands. If the Standard toolbar is *not* visible when you start Explorer, open the View menu, select Toolbars, then select Standard Buttons.

 Moves back through pages previously displayed. Back is available only if you have moved around among Web pages in the current Navigator session; otherwise, it is dimmed.

 Moves forward through pages previously displayed. Forward is available only if you have used the Back button; otherwise, it is dimmed.

 Interrupts the opening of a page that is taking too long to display. Some pages are so filled with graphics, audio, or video clips that delays can be expected.

 Reloads the current page.

 Returns you to your home page. You can change your home page to open to any Web site or a blank page (View, Internet Options, General).

 Allows you to select from a number of search services with a variety of options.

 Displays the Web sites that you have stored using the features available on the Favorites menu. Click Favorites button again to close the Favorites.

Displays links to Web sites that you have visited in previous days and weeks. You can change the number of days that sites are stored in your History folder (View, Internet Options). Click the History button again to close the History window.

 Displays the list of current channels on the Explorer bar. Click again to close the Channels window.

 Conceals Menu, titles, Status bar, and address line to make available the maximum screen space possible for viewing a Web page. Click it again to restore Menu, titles, Status bar, and address line.

 Displays a drop-down menu with various Mail and News options. You will learn about Outlook Express e-mail options in Chapters 10-12.

Open a World Wide Web Site from the Address Bar

■ Click in the Address bar and start typing the address of the Web site you want to open. If you have visited the site before, Internet Explorer will try to complete the address automatically. If it is the correct address, press Enter to go to it. If it is not the correct address, type over the suggested address that displayed on the line. To see other possible matches, click the down arrow. If you find the one you want, click on it.

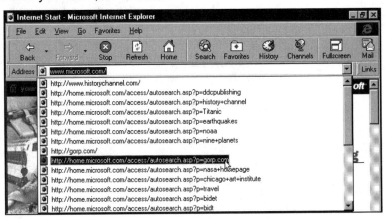

■ To turn off the AutoComplete feature, open the View menu, select Internet Options, and click the Advanced tab. Deselect Use AutoComplete in the Browsing area of the dialog box.

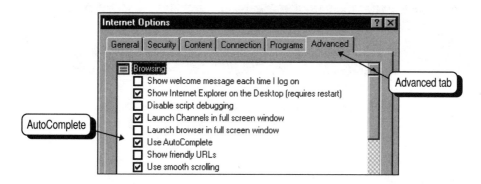

Open a World Wide Web Site Using the File Open Dialog Box

- Select File, Open, and start entering the exact address of the site you want to open. If AutoComplete is turned on and Explorer finds a potential match for the site, it will automatically appear on this line. If the match is the site you want to open, press Enter to go there. If you want to see other possible matches, click the down arrow in the open dialog box.

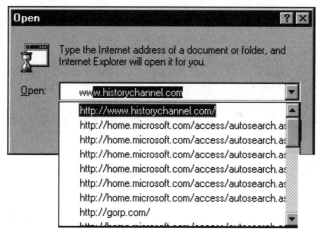

√ *Other ways of opening Web sites will be explored in this lesson. Chapters 19-21 will explain how to search for sites whose exact addresses you do not know.*

Microsoft Internet Explorer: 9

◆ Open and Add to the Favorites Folder
◆ Open Web Sites from the Favorites Folder
◆ Create New Folders in the Favorites Folder
◆ AutoSearch from the Address Bar

Open and Add to the Favorites Folder

■ As you spend more time exploring Web sites, you will find sites that you want to visit frequently. You can store shortcuts to these sites in the **Favorites folder**.

■ To add a site to the Favorites folder, first go to the desired Web site. Open the Favorites menu or right-click anywhere on the page and select Add To Favorites.

■ The following dialog box appears when you select Add to Favorites.

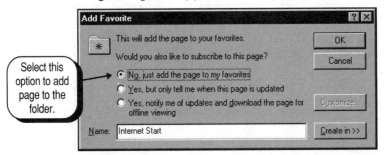

Select this option to add page to the folder.

■ The name of the Page you have opened appears in the Name box. There are three ways you can store the address in response to the question "Would you also like to subscribe to this page?" Subscribing to a page means you can schedule automatic updates to that site.

• No, just add the page to my favorites
Puts a shortcut to the Web site in your Favorites folder.

• Yes, but only tell me when this page is updated
Explorer will alert you when an update to the site is available.

• Yes, notify me of updates and download the page for offline viewing
Explorer will automatically download and update to your computer.

■ Click OK to add the Web address to the Favorites folder.

Open Web Sites from the Favorites Folder

- Click the Favorites button [Favorites] on the Standard toolbar to open Web sites from the Favorites folder. The Explorer bar will open on the left side of the Browser window.

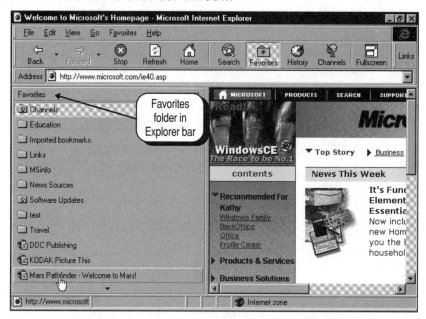

- Click on an address or open a folder and select a site. Close the Explorer bar by clicking the close button or the Favorites button on the toolbar.

- You can also open the Favorites menu and select a site from the list or from a folder.

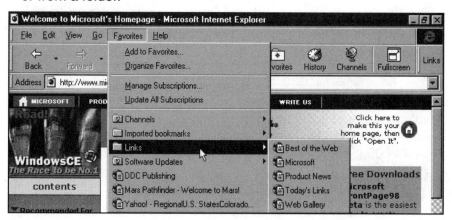

Create New Folders in the Favorites Folder

- You can create new folders before or after you have saved addresses in your Favorites folder.

  - Click Favorites and select Organize Favorites.
  - Click the Create New Folder button (shown in illustration below).

  - Type the name of the new folder and press Enter.

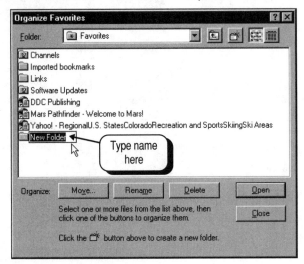

AutoSearch from the Address Bar

- In addition to displaying and entering addresses in the Address bar, you can use AutoSearch to perform a quick search directly from the Address bar.

- Click once in the Address bar and type *go, find,* or *?* and press the spacebar once. Enter the word or phrase you want to find and press Enter. For example, if you want to search for information about the year 2000, type "Find the year 2000" on the Address bar and press Enter.

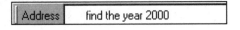

- Note the Status bar displays the message "Finding site..." It is actually finding a search site. In a few moments, the results of your search displays. The keywords in your search appear in bold in the list of links that are relevant to the search string that you entered.

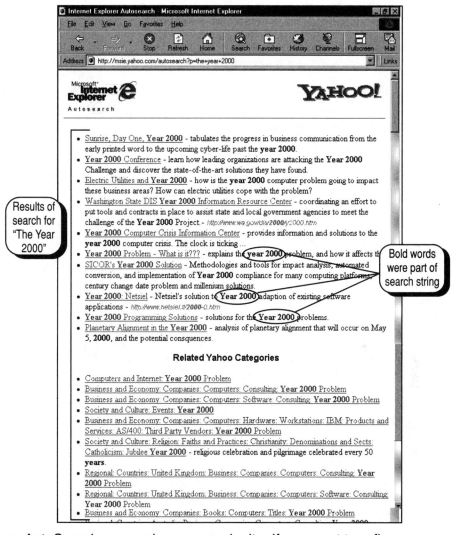

- AutoSearch uses only one search site. If you want to refine your search or see if other search engines will give you different results, click the Search button ⊕ Search on the Standard toolbar and select a Search provider from the Choose provider drop-down list in the Explorer bar to access a different Search site.

◆ **Configure Outlook Express** ◆ **Start Outlook Express**
◆ **Outlook Express Main Window** ◆ **Retrieve New Messages**
◆ **The Mail Window** ◆ **Read Messages** ◆ **Delete a Message**
◆ **Print a Message** ◆ **Save a Message**

Configure Outlook Express

√ *This section assumes that you have already set up an e-mail account with a service provider. If you do not have an e-mail address, contact your Internet Service Provider. Establishing a modem connection and configuring your computer to send and receive mail can be frustrating. Don't be discouraged. What follows are steps that will get you connected, but some of the information may have to be supplied by your Internet Service Provider. Calling for help will save you time and frustration.*

■ Outlook Express is the e-mail program included in the Microsoft Internet Explorer 4.0 suite. With this program, you can send, receive, save, and print e-mail messages and attachments.

■ Before you can use Outlook Express to send and receive e-mail, you must configure the program with your e-mail account information (user name, e-mail address, and mail server names).

■ You may have already filled in this information if you completed the Internet Connection Wizard when you started Internet Explorer for the first time. If not, you can enter the information by running the Internet Connection Wizard again.

Internet Connection Wizard

• Launch Outlook Express. Open the Tools menu, select Accounts. Click the Mail tab. Click Add and select Mail to start the Connection Wizard.

• The Internet Connection Wizard will ask for information necessary to set up or add an e-mail account.

• Enter the name you want to appear on the "From" line in your outgoing messages. Click Next.

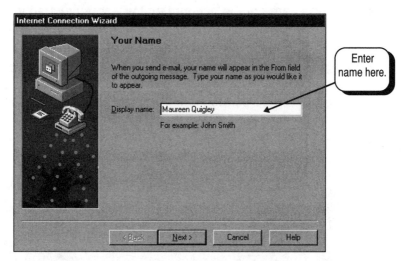

- Type your e-mail address. This is the address that people use to send mail to you. You usually get to create the first part of the address (the portion in front of the @ sign); the rest is assigned by your Internet Service Provider. Click Next.

- Enter the names of your incoming and outgoing mail servers. Check with your Internet Service Provider if you do not know what they are. Click Next.

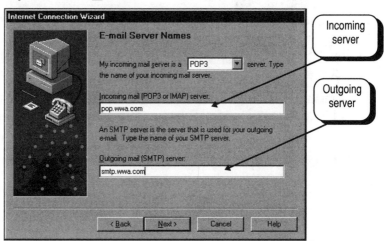

- Enter the logon name that your Internet Service Provider requires for you to access your mail. You will probably also have to enter a password. The password will appear as asterisks (******) to prevent others from knowing it. Click Next when you are finished.

- Enter the name of the account that will appear when you open the Accounts list on the Tools menu in Outlook Express. It can be any name that you choose. Click Next when you have finished.

- Select the type of connection that you are using to reach the Internet. If you are connecting through a phone line, you will need to have a dial-up connection. If you have an existing connection, click Next and select from the list of current connections.

- Select an existing dial-up connection, or select Create a new dial-up connection and follow the directions to create a new one.

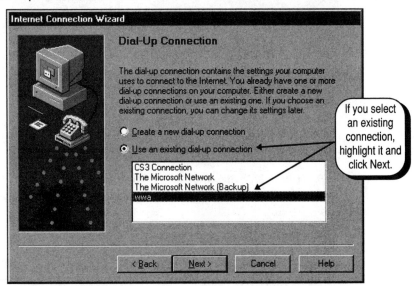

- If you select Use an existing dial-up connection you will click Finish in the last window to save the settings. You should then be able to launch Outlook Express and send and receive mail and attachments.

Start Outlook Express

■ To start Outlook Express:

- Click the Mail icon ![icon] on the taskbar.

  √ There is a chance that clicking the Mail icon from the Explorer main window will take you to the Microsoft Outlook organizational program. To use the more compact Outlook Express as your default mail program, click View, Internet Options from the Explorer main window. Click the Programs tab and choose Outlook Express from the Mail pull-down menu.

  √ If you downloaded Internet Explorer 4, be sure that you downloaded the standard version, which includes Outlook Express in addition to the Web browser.

Outlook Express Main Window

■ After you launch Outlook Express, the main Outlook Express window opens by default. You can access any e-mail function from this window.

Outlook Express Main Window

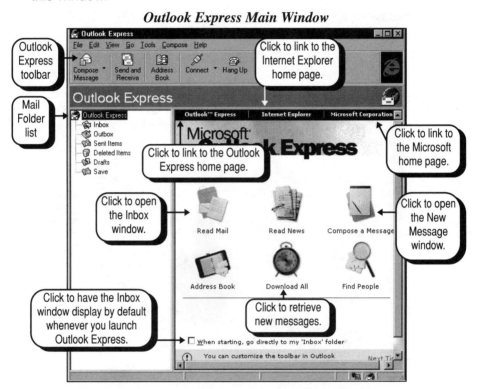

■ Descriptions of items in the main window follow below:

- The **Mail Folder list** displays in the left column of the window, with the Outlook Express main folder selected. To view the contents of a different folder, click on the desired folder in the folder list.

- **Shortcuts** to different e-mail functions are located in the center of the window. Click once on a shortcut to access the indicated task or feature.

- **Hyperlinks** to Microsoft home pages are located at the top of the window. Click once to connect to the indicated home page.

- The **Outlook Express toolbar** displays buttons for commonly used commands. Note that each button contains an image and text that describes the button function. Move your cursor over the button to display specific function information. Clicking any of these buttons will activate the indicated task immediately.

Retrieve New Messages

- You can access the retrieve new mail command from any Outlook Express window. To do so:

  - Click the Send and Receive button 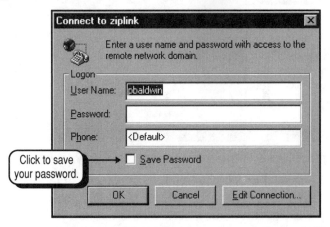 on the toolbar.

- In the Connection dialog box that displays, enter your ISP user name in the User Name text box and your password in the Password text box and click OK. (If you do not know your user name or password, contact your ISP.) Outlook Express will send this information to your ISP's mail server in order to make a connection.

  √ *Outlook Express will automatically save your user name and password for the rest of the current Internet session. However, you must re-enter your password each time you reconnect to the Internet or retrieve new mail, unless you set Outlook Express to save your password permanently. To do so, select the* **Save Password** *check box in the connection dialog box and click OK.*

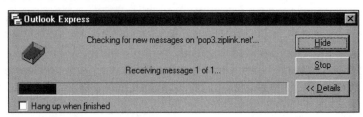

- Once you are connected to the Internet and Outlook Express is connected to your ISP mail server, new mail messages will begin downloading from your ISP mail server. A dialog box displays the status of the transmittal.

The Mail Window

■ After retrieving new messages, Outlook Express stores them in the Inbox folder.

■ To view your new messages, you must open the Mail window and display the contents of the Inbox folder. To do so:

• Click the Read Mail shortcut ![Read Mail] in the Outlook Express main window.

■ The Mail window opens with the Inbox folder displayed. A description of the items in the Mail window appears on the following page:

Mail Window with Inbox Folder Displayed

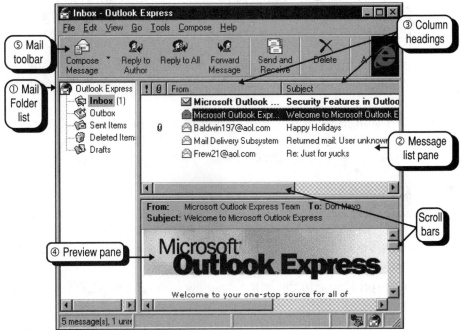

√ *In the message list, unread messages are displayed in bold text with a sealed envelope icon* ![icon] *to the left of the header. Messages that have been read are listed in regular text with an open envelope icon* ![icon] *to the left of the header.*

① The **Mail Folder list** displays the currently selected message folder, the contents of which are displayed in the mail list. Click on another folder to display its contents in the mail list.

② The **message list pane** displays a header for each of the messages contained in the currently selected mail folder.

③ **Column headings** list the categories of information included in each message header, such as subject, from, and date received. You can customize the display of the header columns in a number of ways:

- Resize column widths by placing the mouse pointer over the right border of a column heading until the pointer changes to a double arrow and then click and drag the border to the desired size.

- Rearrange the order of the columns by clicking and dragging a column heading to a new location in the series.

④ The **preview pane** displays the content of the message currently selected from the message list. You can show/hide the preview pane by selecting View, Layout and clicking on the Use preview pane check box. You can resize the preview pane or the message list pane by placing the pointer over the border between the two panes until the pointer changes to a double arrow and then dragging the border up or down to the desired size.

⑤ The **Mail toolbar** displays command buttons for working with messages. These commands vary depending on the message folder currently displayed (Inbox, Sent, Outbox, etc.).

Read Messages

√ *You do not have to be online to read e-mail. You can reduce your online charges if you disconnect from your ISP after retrieving your messages and read them offline.*

- You must have the Mail window open and the mail folder containing the message to read displayed.

- You can read a message in the preview pane of the Mail window, or in a separate window.

- To read a message in the preview pane, click on the desired message header in the message list. If the message does not appear, select View, Layout, Use preview pane.

- To open and read a message in a separate window, double-click on the desired message header in the message list.

  √ *The Message window opens displaying the Message toolbar and the contents of the selected message.*

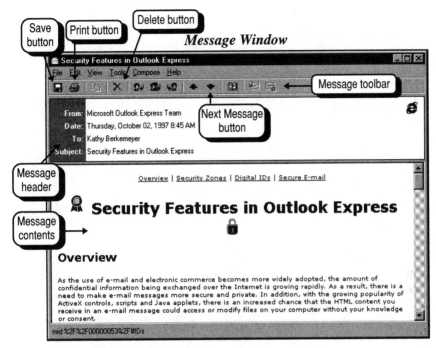

Message Window

- You can close the Message window after reading a message by clicking File, Close or by clicking on the Close button (X) in the upper-right corner of the window.

- Use the scroll bars in the Message window or the preview pane to view hidden parts of a displayed message. Or, press the down arrow key to scroll down through the message.

- To read the next unread message:

  • Select View, Next, Next Unread Message.

  OR

  • If you are viewing a message in the Message window, click the Next button ▼ on the Message toolbar.

- Once you have read a message, it remains stored in the Inbox folder until you delete it or file it in another folder. (See "Delete a Message" on the following page.)

Delete a Message

- To delete a message:
  - Select the desired header from the message list in the Mail window.
  - Click the Delete button in the Mail toolbar, or select Edit, Delete.

    OR
  - Open the desired message in the Message window.
  - Click the Delete button on the Message toolbar.

  √ *To select more than one message to delete, click the Ctrl button while you click each message header.*

Print a Message

- To print a message:
  - Select the message you want to print from the message list in the Mail window or open the message in the Message window.
  - Select Print from the File menu.
  - In the Print dialog box that opens, select the desired print options and click OK.

Print Dialog Box

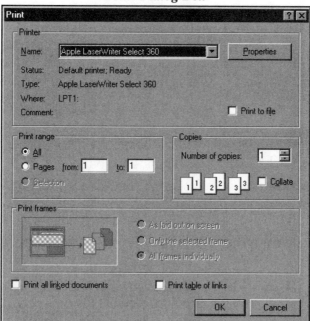

- You can bypass the Print dialog box and send the message to the printer using the most recently used print settings by opening the message in the Message window and clicking the Print button 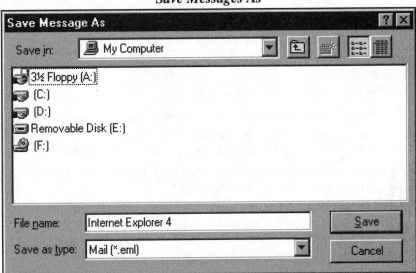 on the Message toolbar.

Save a Message

- To save a message to your hard drive:
  - Open the desired message in the Message window and click the Save button 🖫 on the Message toolbar.
  - In the Save Message As dialog box that opens, click the Save in drop-down list box and select the drive and folder in which to store the message file.

Save Messages As

- Click in the File name box and enter a name for the message.
- Click Save.

Compose New Messages

■ You can compose an e-mail message in Outlook Express while you are connected to the Internet, or while you are offline. When composing an e-mail message online, you can send the message immediately after creating it. When composing a message offline, you will need to store the message in your Outbox folder until you are online and can send it. (See "Send Messages" on page 56.)

■ To create a message, you first need to open the New Message window. To do so:

• Click the New Mail Message button on the toolbar in either the Mail window or the Main window.

The New Message window displays (see the next page).

√ *You can hide any toolbar in the New Message window by going to the View menu and deselecting Toolbar, Formatting Toolbar, or Status Bar.*

• In the New Message window, type the Internet address(es) of the message recipient(s) in the To field.

√ *If you type the first few characters of a name or e-mail address that is saved in your address book, Outlook Express will automatically complete it for you. (See page 60 for information on using the Address Book.)*

OR

Click the Index Card icon in the To field or the Address Book button on the New Message toolbar and select an address to insert (see page 60 for information on using the Address Book).

√ *If you are sending the message to multiple recipients, insert a comma or semicolon between each recipient's address.*

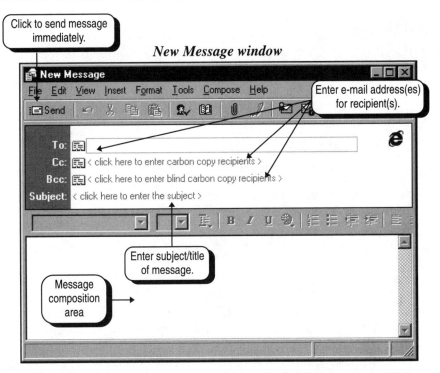

New Message window

- After inserting the address(es) in the To field, you may click in either of the following fields and enter the recipient information indicated.

CC (Carbon Copy)	The e-mail addresses of people who will receive copies of the message.
BCC (Blind Carbon Copy)	Same as CC, except these names will not appear anywhere in the message, so other recipients will not know that the person(s) listed in the BCC field received a copy.

- Click in the Subject field and type the subject of the message. An entry in this field is required.

- Click in the blank composition area below the Subject field and type the body of your message. Wordwrap occurs automatically, and you can cut and paste quotes from other messages or text from other programs. You can also check the spelling of your message by selecting Spelling from the Tools menu and responding to the prompts that follow.

Send Messages

■ Once you have created a message, you have three choices:
  • to send the message immediately
  • to store the message in the Outbox folder to be sent later
  • to save the message in the Drafts folder to be edited and sent later

To send a message immediately:

√ *To be able to send messages immediately, you must first select Options from the Tools menu in the Mail window. Then click on the Send tab and select the Send messages immediately check box. If this option is not selected, clicking the Send button will not send a message immediately, but will send the message to your Outbox until you perform the Send and Receive task.*

  • Click the send button [≣ Send] on the New Message toolbar.
  OR
  Click File, Send Message.

  • Outlook Express then connects to your ISP's mail server and sends out the new message. If the connection to the mail server is successful, the sending mail icon displays in the lower-right corner of the status bar until the transmittal is complete:

  • Sometimes, however, Outlook Express cannot immediately connect to the mail server and instead has to store the new message in the Outbox for later delivery. When this happens, the sending mail icon does not appear, and the number next to your Outbox folder increases by one [·⊗ **Outbox** (1)].

  • Outlook Express does not automatically reattempt to send a message after a failed connection. Instead, you need to manually send the message from the Outbox (see "To send messages from your Outbox folder" on page 57).

To store a message in your Outbox folder for later delivery:

  • Select File, Send Later in the New Message window.

  • The Send Mail prompt displays, telling you that the message will be stored in our Outbox folder.

  • Click OK.

  • The message is saved in the Outbox.

To send messages from your Outbox folder:

- Click on the Send and Receive button 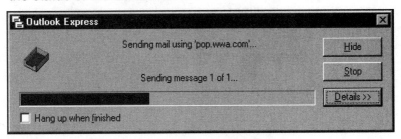 on the toolbar.

  OR

- Click <u>T</u>ools, <u>S</u>end and Receive, All Accounts.

  √ *When you use the Send and Receive command, Outlook Express sends out **all** messages stored in the Outbox and automatically downloads any new mail messages from the mail server.*

- After you click Send and Receive, a dialog box opens, displaying the status of the transmittal.

To save a message to your Drafts folder:

- Click <u>F</u>ile, <u>S</u>ave.
- The Saved Message prompt displays. Click OK.

To edit and send message drafts:

- In the Mail window, click in the Drafts folder **Drafts** (1) from the Mail Folder list.

- Double-click on the desired message header from the message list.

- In the New Message window that appears, edit your message as necessary. When you are finished, select <u>F</u>ile, S<u>e</u>nd Message to send the message immediately, or Eile, Send Later to store it in the Outbox folder for later delivery.

- Outlook Express automatically saves all sent messages in the Sent Items folder. To view a list of the messages you have sent, select the Sent Items folder ⌐📁 Sent Items from the Mail Folder list. The contents will display in the message list pane.

Reply to Mail

- In Outlook Express, you can reply to a message automatically, without having to enter the recipient's name or e-mail address.

- When replying, you have a choice of replying to the author and all recipients of the original message or to the author only.

- To reply to the author and all recipients:
  - Select the message you want to reply to from the message list in the Mail window.
  - Click the Reply to All button 📧 Reply to All on the Mail toolbar.
    OR
  - Right-click on the selected message and select Reply to All.

- To reply to the author only:
  - Click the Reply to Author button 📧 Reply to Author on the Mail toolbar.
    OR
  - Right-click on the selected message and select Reply to Author.

- Once you have selected a reply command, the New Message window opens with the address fields and the Subject filled in for you.

  √ *You can access all of the mail send commands by right-clicking on the message in the Message list.*

- The original message is automatically included in the body of your response. To turn off this default insertion, select Options from the Tools menu, click on the Send tab, deselect the Include message in reply check box, and click OK.

- To compose your reply, click in the composition area and type your text as you would in a new message.

- When you are done, click the Send button ⌐≡Send⌐ on the New Message toolbar to send the message immediately. Or, select Send Later from the File menu to store the message in the Outbox folder for later delivery. To save the reply as a draft to be edited and sent later, select Save from the File menu.

Forward Mail

- To forward a message automatically without having to enter the message subject:

  • Select the message to forward from the message list in the Mail window.

  • Click the Forward Message button ⌐⌐ on the Mail toolbar.

    The New Message window opens with the original message displayed and the Subject field filled in for you.

- Fill in the e-mail address information by either typing each address or selecting the recipients from your address book. (See "Address a New Message Using the Personal Address Book" on page 62.)

  √ *If you are forwarding the message to multiple recipients, insert a comma or semicolon between each recipient's address.*

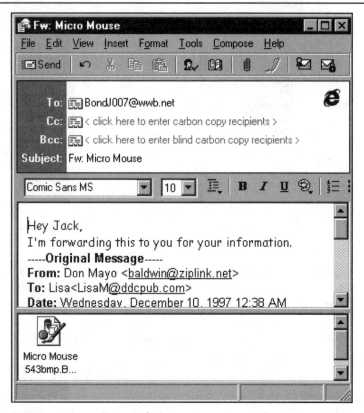

- Click in the composition area and type any text you wish to send with the forwarded message.

- When you are done, click the Send button ![Send] on the New Message toolbar to send the message immediately. Or, select Send Later from the File menu to store the message in the Outbox folder for later delivery. To save the reply as a draft to be edited and sent later, select Save from the File menu.

Add Entries to the Personal Address Book

- In Outlook Express, you can use the Windows Address Book to store e-mail addresses and other information about your most common e-mail recipients. You can then use the Address Book to find and automatically insert addresses when creating new messages.

- To open the Windows Address Book:

  - Click the Address Book button ![Address Book] on the toolbar in the Mail window or the Main window.

The Address Book window opens, displaying a list of contacts.

Address Book Window

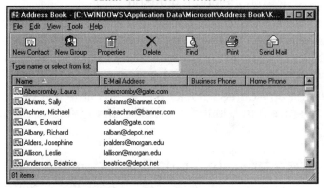

- To add a name to the address book:

  - Click the New Contact button ![New Contact] on the Address Book toolbar.

  - In the Properties dialog box that displays, type the First, Middle and Last names of the new contact in the appropriate text boxes.

  - Type the contact's e-mail address in the Add new text box and then click the Add button. You can repeat this procedure if you wish to list additional e-mail addresses for the contact.

  - In the Nickname text box, you can enter a nickname for the contact (the nickname must be unique among the entries in your address book). When addressing a new message, you can type the nickname in the To field, rather than typing the entire address, and Outlook Express will automatically complete the address.

Contact Properties Dialog Box

- You can automatically add the name and address of the sender of a message by opening the message in the Message window, right-clicking on the sender's name in the To field, and selecting Add to Address Book from the shortcut menu.

- You can also set Outlook Express to add the address of recipients automatically when you reply to a message. To do so, select Options from the Tools menu and select the Automatically put people I reply to in my Address Book check box on the General tab.

- You can edit an Address Book entry at any time by double-clicking on the person's name in the contact list in the Address Book window.

Address a New Message Using the Personal Address Book

- To insert an address from your address book into a new message:

  - Click the Select Recipients button [icon] on the New Message toolbar.

  - In the Select Recipients dialog box that follows, select the address to insert from the contact list.

Select Recipients Dialog Box

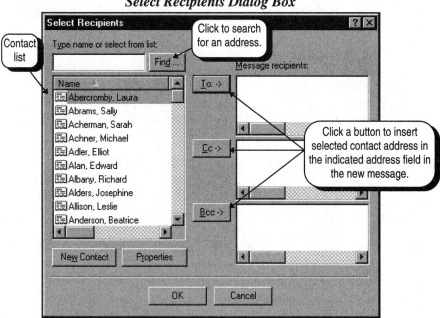

  - Click the button for the field in which you want to insert the address (To, Cc, or Bcc). Click OK to return to the New Message window when you are finished.

Outlook Express: 12

◆ **View Attached Files** ◆ **Save Attached Files** ◆ **Attach Files to a Message**

View Attached Files

- Sometimes an e-mail message will come with a separate file(s) attached. Messages containing attachments are indicated in the message list in the Mail window by a paperclip icon 🔋 to the left of the message header.

- If the selected message is displayed in the preview pane, a larger paper clip attachment icon will appear to the right of the header at the top of the preview pane.

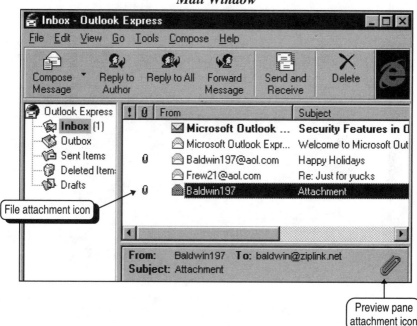

Mail Window

- If you open the selected message in its own window, an attachment icon will appear in a separate pane below the message.

- To view an attachment:
  - Open the folder containing the desired message in the Mail window.
  - Select the message containing the desired attachment(s) from the message list to display it in the preview pane.

  If the attachment is an image, it will display in the message.

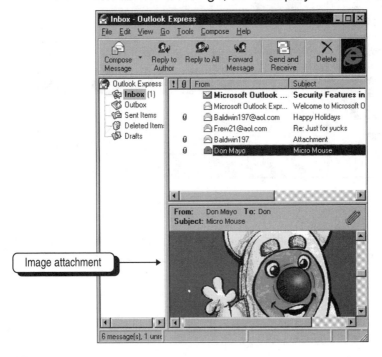

√ *If the image does not display, click Tools, Options, click the Read tab, select the Automatically show picture attachments in messages check box, and click OK.*

■ Other types of attachments, such as a program, word processor document, or media clip, do not display in the message, but have to be opened in a separate window. To do so:

• Click on the attachment icon 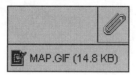 in the preview pane. A button will display with the file name and size of the attachment.

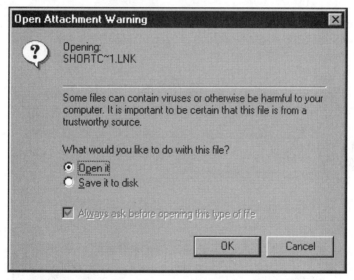

• Click on this button.

• If the Open Attachment Warning dialog box displays, select the Open it option and click OK.

■ Outlook Express will open the attached file or play the attached media clip.

■ If the attached file does not open, Outlook Express does not recognize the file type of the attached file (that is, Outlook Express does not contain the plug-in, or your computer does not contain the application needed to view it).

■ To view an unrecognized attachment, you have to install and/or open the application or plug-in needed to view it.

Save Attached Files

- If desired, you can save an attached file to your hard drive or disk for future use or reference. To save an attachment:

  - Select Save Attachments from the File menu, and select the attachment to save from the submenu that displays.

  OR

  - Right-click on the attachment icon  in the Message window and select the Save As option.

  - In the Save As dialog box that follows, click the Save in drop-down list box and select the drive and folder in which to save the file.

    Save As Dialog Box

  - Click in the File name text box and type a name for the file.
  - Click Save.

Attach Files to a Message

■ You can attach a file to an e-mail message while composing the message in the New Message window. To add an attachment:

- Click the Attachments button 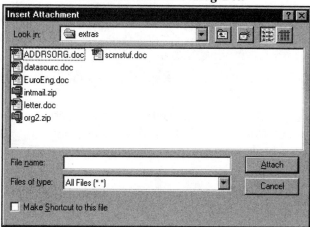 on the New Message toolbar.
  OR
- Click Insert, File Attachment.
- In the Insert Attachment dialog box that appears, click the Look in drop-down list box and select the drive and folder containing the file to attach. Then select the file and click Attach.

Insert Attachment Dialog Box

√ *The attachment will appear as an icon in the body of the message.*

√ *Messages containing attachments usually take longer to send than those without attachments.*

√ *When attaching very large files or multiple files, you may want to zip (compress) the files before attaching them. To do so, both you and the recipient need a file compression program, such as WinZip or PKZip.*

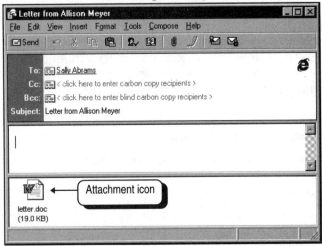

New Message Dialog Box

- You can also attach a file by dragging the desired file from your desktop or from Windows Explorer into the New Message window.

- You can add multiple attachments by repeating the procedure as many times as you like.

- Before you send a message containing an attachment, you may wish to make sure the recipient's e-mail program can decode the file you are sending.

America Online: 13

◆ About America Online ◆ Start America Online
◆ The AOL Home Page, Menu, and Toobar ◆ AOL Help ◆ Exit AOL

About America Online?

- America Online (AOL) is an all-purpose online service. Unlike Netscape Navigator or Microsoft Internet Explorer, AOL is not an Internet browser, yet you can browse the Internet using AOL navigation features.

- Unlike Internet browsers, AOL does not require a separate Internet Service provider for Internet access, nor does it require a separate mail server connection to access e-mail from the AOL Mail Center. When you install AOL, you configure the program to establish a dial-up connection to the AOL server using your modem. All connections to the Internet and the Mail Center are made via the AOL server.

  √ *An Internet service provider is a company that provides Internet access.*

Start America Online

- To start America Online (Windows 95):

  - Click the AOL icon on your desktop. This icon should display on your desktop after you install AOL.

    OR

    Click the Start button, Programs, America Online, America Online for Windows 95.

  - Make sure your screen name is displayed in the Select Screen Name box and type in your password in the Enter Password box.

  - Click the Sign On button SIGN ON to connect to the AOL server.

The AOL Home Page, Menu, and Toolbar

- After you successfully log on to America Online, you will see a series of screens. The final first screen you see is the AOL home page or start page. The AOL home page contains links to daily AOL featured areas as well as links to constant AOL areas such as *Channels* and *What's New*. You can also access your mailbox from the home page.

Home Screen Menu

- The AOL menu displays options currently available. Click the heading to display a drop-down menu of links to AOL areas and basic filing, editing, and display options.

America Online Toolbar

- The AOL toolbar contains buttons for AOL's most commonly used commands. Choosing a button activates the indicated task immediately.

	You have new mail if the flag on the mailbox is in the up position. Click to display a list of new mail in your mailbox.
	Compose and Send Mail Messages. Displays the Composition screen for composing new mail messages.

	Channels are areas of interest arranged by category. AOLs 21 channels offer hundreds of AOL areas and Web site connections.
	New and exciting AOL areas to explore including new AOL features, areas, and special interest sites.
	People Connection takes you to the AOL chat area. Here you can access the AOL Community Center, Chat Rooms, and meet the stars in the Live chat forum.
	File Search opens the search window to the software library where you can download hundreds of software programs.
	Stocks and Portfolios links you to the latest stock market quotes, research a company or mutual fund, or find the latest financial news.
	This area not only brings you the latest headline news, weather, and sports but also allows you to search news archives by keywords. You can also see multimedia (slide show and audio) presentations of the hottest topics in the news.
	Connects you to the Web.
	Shop Online in the AOL Marketplace. Goods and services are categorized for your convenience.
	Lets you customize AOL to suit your needs. Each member area shows you step-by-step how to access and select options.
	Click to see an estimate of how long you have been online for the current session.
	Click to print whatever is displayed on your computer screen. Opens the Print dialog box where you can select from the standard print options.
	The Personal Filing Cabinet is a storage area located on your hard disk used to organize files such as downloaded e-mail messages, files, and newsgroup messages.
	Click this icon to create links or shortcuts to your favorite Web sites or AOL areas.
	This is a quick way to access the AOL member directory and to find answers to questions.
	Displays an area called Find Central. Go here to search the AOL directory using keywords and phrases.
	Each AOL area has a keyword to identify the area. Enter the Keyword for immediate access to the desired AOL area.

AOL Help

■ AOL offers extensive Help so that you can learn to use AOL effectively and find answers to any questions you may have about either AOL or the Web. All AOL topics can be printed or saved to your hard disk.

■ To access Help, click Help and the help topic of choice from the menu.

Exit AOL

■ To exit AOL, click the close window button [X] in the upper-right corner of the AOL screen.

OR

Click Sign Off, Sign Off on the menu bar.

OR

Click File, Exit.

◆ **Access the Internet from AOL** ◆ **Open a Wold Wide Web Site**
◆ **The AOL Browser Screen** ◆ **Stop a Load or Search**

Access the Internet from AOL

■ To go to the Internet Connection:

- Click the Internet button 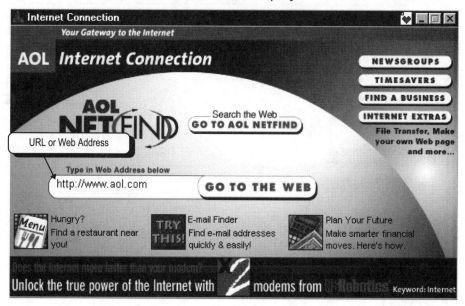 on the AOL main screen.

  OR

- Click **internet** from the Channels menu.

  OR

- Press Ctrl+K, type internet in the Keyword box and press Enter. *The Internet Connection window displays.*

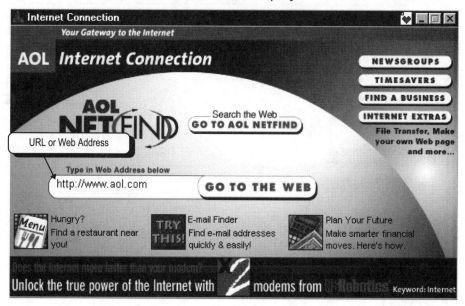

Open a World Wide Web Site

- If you know the Web address (URL), type it into the Type in Web Address below box and click the GO TO THE WEB button **GO TO THE WEB** or press Enter. If the Web address is correct, you will be connected to the Web site.

- If you wish to search the Internet, click the GO TO AOL NETFIND button **GO TO AOL NETFIND**.
  Search the Web

The AOL Browser Screen

- Once you are connected to the Web, the screen elements change, and the Browser toolbar displays.

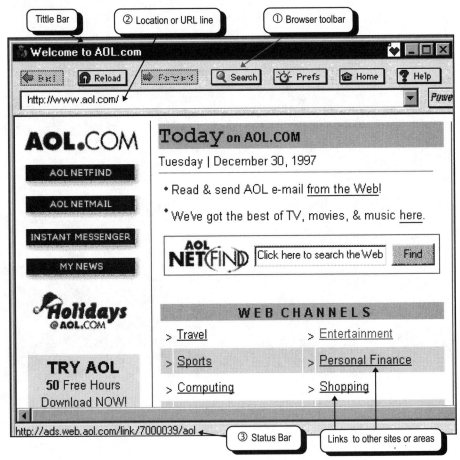

① **Browser Toolbar**

- The AOL Browser toolbar will help you navigate through sites you visit on the Web. Buttons on the Browser toolbar also connect you to search and Internet preference areas.

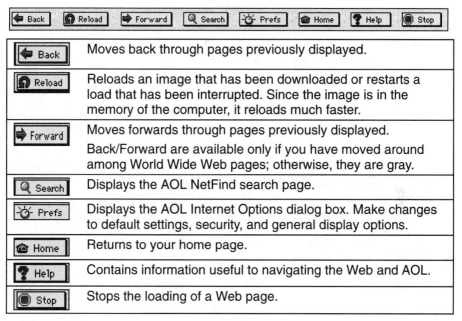

Back	Moves back through pages previously displayed.
Reload	Reloads an image that has been downloaded or restarts a load that has been interrupted. Since the image is in the memory of the computer, it reloads much faster.
Forward	Moves forwards through pages previously displayed. Back/Forward are available only if you have moved around among World Wide Web pages; otherwise, they are gray.
Search	Displays the AOL NetFind search page.
Prefs	Displays the AOL Internet Options dialog box. Make changes to default settings, security, and general display options.
Home	Returns to your home page.
Help	Contains information useful to navigating the Web and AOL.
Stop	Stops the loading of a Web page.

② **Location Line**

- AOL stores each Web address you visit during each AOL session. If you wish to return to an address you have visited during the current session, you can click the location box arrow and click the address from the pull-down list.

③ Status Bar

- The Status bar, located at the bottom of the screen, is a helpful indicator of the progress of the loading of a Web page. For example, if you are loading a Web site, you will see the byte size of the page, the percentage of the task completed, and the number of graphics and links yet to load. In many cases the time it will take to load the page will display.

Stop a Load or Search

- Searching for information or loading a Web page can be time-consuming, especially if the Web page has many graphic images, if a large number of people are trying to access the site at the same time, or if your modem and computer operate at slower speeds. If data is taking a long time to load, you may wish to stop a search or the loading of a page or large file.

- To stop a search or load:
  - Click the Stop button ⬛ Stop on the Navigation toolbar.

- If you decide to continue the load after clicking the Stop button, click the Reload button ⬛ Reload.

Favorite Places

- A **Favorite Place** listing is a bookmark that you create containing the title, URL, and a direct link to a Web page or AOL area that you may want to revisit. A Favorite Place listings links directly to the desired page.

- The AOL Favorite Place feature allows you to maintain a record of Web sites in your Favorite Places file so that you can return to them easily. (See "Add Favorite Places" below.)

Add Favorite Places

- There are several ways to mark an AOL area or Web site and save it as a Favorite Place. Once the page is displayed:

  - Click the Favorite Place heart 🖤 on the Web site or AOL area title bar.

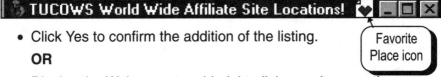

  - Click Yes to confirm the addition of the listing.

    OR

    Favorite
    Place icon

  - Display the Web page to add, right-click anywhere on the page and select Add to Favorites from the shortcut menu.

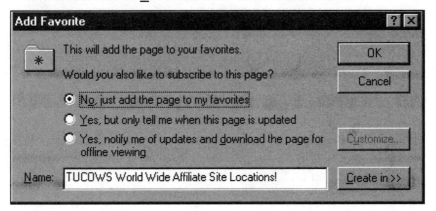

- Click the desired option from the confirmation box that displays and click OK.
- The site will automatically be added to your Favorite Places list.

View Favorite Places

■ You can view the Favorite Places file by selecting Go To, Favorite Places, or by clicking on the Favorite Places button on the AOL toolbar. Click on any listing from the list to go directly to that page.

■ The details of any Favorite Place listing can be viewed or modified by using the buttons on the Favorite Places screen.

Delete Favorite Places

■ You may wish to delete a Favorite Place if a Web site no longer exists or remove an AOL area from the listing that is no longer of interest to you.

To delete a Favorite Place:

- Click the Favorite Places button on the toolbar.
- Click on the listing to delete.
- Click the Delete button **Delete** from the Favorite Places screen.
  OR
- Right-click on the listing and select Delete from the pop-up menu.
  OR
- Press the Delete key.
- Click YES to confirm the deletion.

AOL History List

■ While you move back and forth within a Web site, AOL automatically records each page location. The history is only temporary and is deleted when you sign-off. AOL areas are not recorded in the history list.

■ To view the history list, click on the arrow at the end of the URL line. You can use History to jump back or forward to recently viewed pages by clicking on the page from the list.

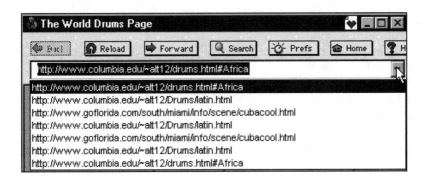

Save Web Pages

- When you find a Web page with information that you would like to keep for future reference, or to review later offline, you can save it to your hard disk. To save a Web page:

  - Click File, Save
  - Type a filename in the File name box.

    √ When you save a Web page, often the current page name appears in the File name box. You can use this name or type a new one.

  - Choose the drive and folder in which to store the file from the Save in drop-down list
  - Click Save.

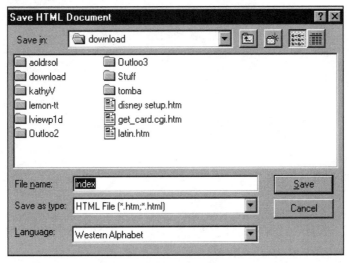

- In most cases when you choose to save a Web page, AOL will automatically save it as an HTML file. Saving a page as an HTML file saves the original formatting and, when accessed, will display as you saw it on the Web.

- You can also save a Web page as a Plain text file which saves only the page text without the formatting or images and placeholders. You might want to do this when saving a very large file, such as a literary work or multiple-page article. To save in Plain text format, click the down arrow next to the Save as type box in the Save As dialog box and select Plain text from the list.

- You can view a saved Web page later by clicking File, Open, and entering the name and location from the Open a File box or by choosing the location and double-clicking on the file name.

Print Web Pages

- One of the many uses of the Internet is to find and print information. You can print a page as it appears on screen, or you can print it as plain text. Only displayed pages can be printed. To print a Web page, display it and do the following:

  - Click the Print button on the AOL toolbar.

    OR

  - Click Print on the File menu.

  - In the Print dialog box that displays, select the desired print options and click OK.

- In most cases, the Web page will be printed in the format shown in the Web page display.

◆ Read New Mail ◆ Compose a New Mail Message
◆ Send Messages ◆ Reply to Mail
◆ Forward Mail ◆ AOL Mail Help

Read New Mail

■ There are several ways to know whether you have new mail in your mailbox: If your computer has a sound card and speakers, you will hear "You've Got Mail" when you successfully connect to AOL. The link is replaced by the You Have Mail link, and the mailbox icon on the main screen has the flag in the up position .

To display and read new and unread mail:

• Click the You Have Mail button on the AOL main screen.
OR

• Click the Read New Mail button 🖳 on the main screen toolbar
OR

• Press Ctrl+R.

  √ *The New Mail list displays new and unread mail for the screen name used for this session. If you have more than one screen name, you must sign on under each name to retrieve new mail.*

  √ *New and Unread e-mail messages remain on the AOL mail server for approximately 27 days before being deleted by AOL. If you want to save a message to your hard disk, click **File, Save As** and choose a location for the message. By default the message will be saved to the Download folder.*

• To read a message, double-click on it from the New Mail list.

Compose a New Mail Message

• Click Mail, Compose Mail.
OR

• Click the Compose Mail button 🖼 on the main screen toolbar.
OR

• Click Ctrl+M.

The Compose Mail screen displays.

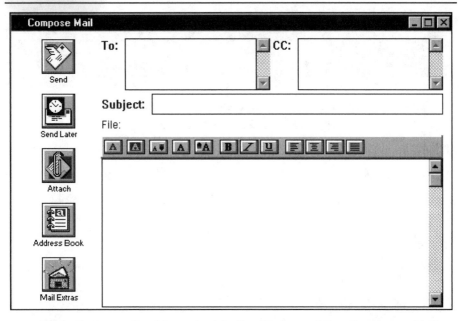

- Fill in the e-mail address(es) in the To box of the Compose Mail screen.

  OR

- Select Address Book and double-click to select an address. (See "America Online E-mail: 18" on page 88 for more information on your Address book.)

- If you are sending the same message to multiple recipients, fill in the CC: (Carbon Copy) box with the e-mail addresses of recipients who will receive a copy of this message. These names will display to all recipients of the message.

- If you want to send BCC: (Blind courtesy copies—copies of a message sent to others but whose names are not visible to the main or other recipients), put the address in parenthesis, for example: (ddcpub.com).

  √ *Multiple addresses must be separated with a comma.*

- Fill in the Subject box with a one-line summary of your message. AOL will not deliver a message without a subject heading. This is the first thing the recipient sees in the list of new mail when your message is delivered.

- Fill in the body of the message.

Send Messages

- Click the Send button [Send] to send the message immediately. *You must be online.*

  OR

- Click the Send Later button [Send Later] to send a message later that you have composed offline.

Reply to Mail

- You can reply to mail messages while online or compose replies to e-mail offline to send later.

- To reply to e-mail:

  - Click the Reply button [Reply] from the displayed message screen. If the message has been sent to more than one person, you can send your response to each recipient of the message by clicking the Reply to All button [Reply to All]. The addresses of the sender and, if desired, all recipients will be automatically inserted into the address fields.

    √ *To include part or all of the original message in your Reply, select the contents of the original message to be included in quotes in your message and click the Reply button to begin your reply.*

  - Click the Send button [Send] if you are online and want to send the reply immediately or click the Send Later button [Send Later].

Forward Mail

■ There are times when you may want to send mail sent to you on to someone else.

■ To forward e-mail:

● Click the Forward button from the displayed message screen and fill in the address(es) of the recipients of the forwarded message. The Subject heading from the original message is automatically inserted into the subject heading box.

● Click the Send button if you are online and want to send

the reply immediately or click the Send Later button .

AOL Mail Help

■ For answers to many of your basic e-mail questions, click Mail, Mail

Center, and click on the Let's Get Started button .

◆ **Add Attachments to a Message**
◆ **Download File Attachments**

Add Attachments to a Message

■ You can attach a file to send along with any e-mail message. Before you send a file attachment—especially if it is a multimedia file—it is a good idea to make sure that the recipient's e-mail program can read the attachment. For example, files sent in MIME format cannot be viewed by AOL e-mail and require separate software to be opened.

To attach files to a message:

• Compose the message to be sent. (See "Compose a New Mail Message" on page 81.)

• Click the Attach button [Attach] on the Compose Message screen.

• Select the drive and folder where the file you wish to attach is located.

• Double-click the file to attach from the Attach File dialog box.

  √ *The attachment will appear below the Subject box.*

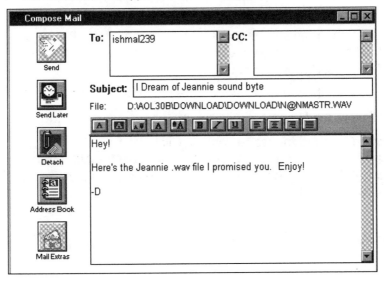

- If you are online, click the Send button [Send] to send the

 message immediately, or click the Send Later button [Send Later] to store the message in your Outgoing Mail if you are working offline.

 √ *Multiple files must be grouped together in a single archive using a file compression program such as PKZIP or WINZIP. Both you and the recipient will need a file compression program.*

Download E-mail File Attachments

■ An e-mail message that arrives with a file attachment is displayed in your new mail list with a small diskette under the message icon.

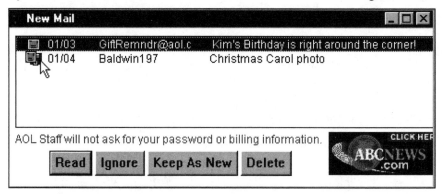

■ Opening the message and viewing the attachment are two separate steps:

- Open the message by double-clicking on it from the New Mail list (see "To display and read new and unread mail" on page 81). The message will display.

- You can choose to download the file attachment immediately by clicking the Download File button [Download File] at the bottom of the displayed message screen. Click the Save button [Save] on the Download Manager screen to save the file, by default, to the AOL30/Download folder. If you desire, you can change the save destination folder.

- A status box will display while the attachment is being downloaded or transferred to your computer.

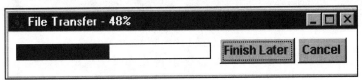

- At the end of the download, the file transfer box will close and you will see the message "File's Done."

OR

- You may choose to download the file later. Click the Download Later button **Download Later** to store the message in the Download Manager. When you are ready to download the file, click File, Download Manager, and then select the file to download. You must be online.

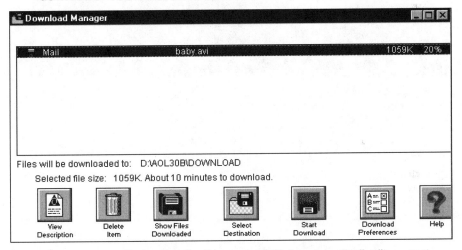

√ *Click Sign off after transfer if you want AOL to automatically disconnect when the transfer is complete.*

To change the default location of where files are stored:

- Click the Select Destination button ![Select Destination] from the Download Manager screen and choose the desired destination from the Select Path dialog box.

◆ **Add Entries to the Address Book**
◆ **Enter an Address Using the Address Book**

Add Entries to the Address Book

■ Once you start sending e-mail, you may be surprised at how many people you start to communicate with online. An easy way to keep track of e-mail addresses is to enter them into the Address Book. Once an e-mail address entry has been created, you can automatically insert it from the Address Book into the address fields.

To create Address Book entries:

• Click <u>M</u>ail, Edit <u>A</u>ddress Book. The Address Book dialog box displays.

• Click the Create button [**Create**] to open the Address Group box.

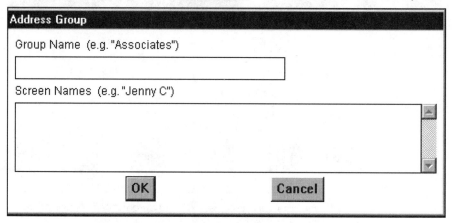

• Enter the real name or nickname of the e-mail recipient (e.g., JohnV) or the name of a Group listing (e.g., Book Club) in the Group Name box. The name you enter in this box is the name that will appear in the Address Book list.

• Press the Tab key to move to the Screen Names box and enter the complete e-mail address of the recipient or the e-mail addresses of everyone in the group listing. When entering multiple addresses such as in a group listing, each address must be separated by a comma (e.g., Baldwin168, BubbaB@ziplink.net, etc.).

- Click OK.

  √ *When sending mail to AOL members through AOL, you do not need to enter the @aol.com domain information. Enter only their screen name as the e-mail address. For all other Address Book entries you must enter the entire address.*

Delete an Address Book Entry

- Click <u>M</u>ail, Edit <u>A</u>ddress Book to open the Address Book.

- Click the name to delete.

- Click the Delete button | Delete |.

- Click Yes.

- Click OK to close the Address Book.

Enter an Address Using the Address Book

- Place the cursor in the desired address field.

- Click the Address Book button [Address Book] to open the Address Book.

- Double-click the name or names from the Address Book list to insert in the TO: or CC: address box and click OK.

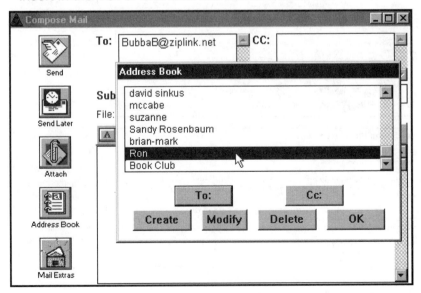

◆ **Searching vs. Surfing** ◆ **Search Sites** ◆ **Search Basics**

Searching vs. Surfing

- The Web is a vast source of information, but to find information that you want, you must be able to locate it. The Web has many thousands of locations, containing hundreds of thousands of pages of information.

- Unlike libraries that use either the Library of Congress or Dewey Decimal system to catalog information, the Internet has no uniform way of tracking and indexing information. You can find lots of information on the Internet; the trick is to find information that you want. Initially, it may seem easy to find information on the Web— you just connect to a relevant site and then start clicking on links to related sites. Illustrated below is an example of a search that starts out on one topic and ends on an unrelated one.

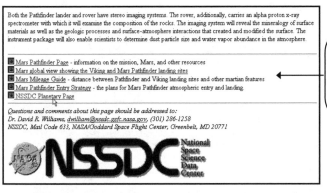

Both the Pathfinder lander and rover have stereo imaging systems. The rover, additionally, carries an alpha proton x-ray spectrometer with which it will examine the composition of the rocks. The imaging system will reveal the mineralogy of surface materials as well as the geologic processes and surface-atmosphere interactions that created and modified the surface. The instrument package will also enable scientists to determine dust particle size and water vapor abundance in the atmosphere.

- Mars Pathfinder Page - information on the mission, Mars, and other resources
- Mars global view showing the Viking and Mars Pathfinder landing sites
- Mars Mileage Guide - distance between Pathfinder and Viking landing sites and other martian features
- Mars Pathfinder Entry Strategy - the plans for Mars Pathfinder atmospheric entry and landing
- NSSDC Planetary Page

Questions and comments about this page should be addressed to:
Dr. David R. Williams, dwilliam@nssdc.gsfc.nasa.gov, (301) 286-1258
NSSDC, Mail Code 633, NASA/Goddard Space Flight Center, Greenbelt, MD 20771

NSSDC National Space Science Data Center

This Web site contains links to sites about the Mars Pathfinder mission. Click on the link to the National Space Science Data Center.

What's New in Planetary Science

Results of the Mars Pathfinder mission, including a mission summary and APXS Mars surface composition results have been published in *Science* magazine.

- The Mars Global Surveyor resumed its aerobraking activities on November 7th following an analysis of the condition of the solar panels by the project. More detail is available in the NASA press release from the press conference held on 10 November.

- The first 14 volumes of the Clementine Lunar Digital Image Model CD-ROMs are now available from NSSDC. These volumes are regional mosaics created from Clementine images showing the Moon at a resolution of 100 meters/pixel. Volume 15 has lower resolution global views and is expected at the end of 1997.

- Upcoming Planetary Events and Missions
- New and Incoming Planetary Data at NSSDC
- New and Updated Planetary Pages

This Web site contains links to sites that have broader information about space exploration. Click on the link to Upcoming Planetary Events and Missions.

Upcoming Planetary Events and Missions

Upcoming Planetary Launches and Events

1997 December 16 - <u>Galileo</u> - Europa closest flyby

1998 January 6 - <u>Lunar Prospector</u> - Launch of NASA Global Orbiter Mission to the Moon
1998 January 23 - <u>NEAR</u> - Earth Flyby
1998 April 26 - <u>Cassini</u> - Venus-1 Flyby
1998 July - <u>New Millenium Deep Space-1</u> - Launch of NASA Flyby Mission to Asteroid 3352 McAuliffe and Comet
P/West-Kohoutek-Ikemura
1998 August 6 - <u>Planet-B</u> - Launch of ISAS (Japan) Orbiter Mission to Mars
1998 December - <u>Mars Surveyor '98 Orbiter</u> - Launch of NASA Orbiter Mission to Mars

Click on Cassini link to go to a Web site that deals with a project to explore Saturn.

Cassini

Cassini has launched!

Launch Date/Time: 15 October 1997 at 08:43 UTC
Launch Vehicle: Titan IV-Centaur
Planned on-orbit mass: 2175 Kg
Power System: Radioisotope Thermal Generators (RTGs) of 630 W

The Cassini Orbiter's mission consists of delivering a probe (called <u>Huygens</u>, provided by ESA) to Titan, and then remaining in orbit around Saturn for detailed studies of the planet and its rings and satellites. The principal objectives are to: (1) determine the three-dimensional structure and dynamical behavior of the rings; (2) determine the composition of the satellite surfaces and

- This is the stream of consciousness method of searching the Internet (**surfing**). It may be interesting and fun to locate information this way, but there are drawbacks. Surfing randomly for information is time consuming and the results are frequently inconsistent and incomplete. It can also be expensive if you are charged fees for connect time to your Internet Service Provider.

- If you want a more systematic and organized way of looking for information, you can connect to one of several search sites that use **search engines** to track, catalog, and index information on the Internet.

Search Sites

- A **search site** builds its catalog using a search engine. A search engine is a software program that goes out on the Web, seeking Web sites, and cataloging them, usually by downloading their home pages.

- Search sites are classified by the way they gather Web site information. All search sites use a search engine in one way or another to gather information. Below is an explanation of how the major search services assemble and index information.

Search Engines

- A search site builds its catalog using a **search engine**. A search engine is a software program that goes out on the Web, seeking Web sites, and cataloging them, usually by downloading their home pages.

- Search engines are sometimes called **spiders** or **crawlers** because they crawl the Web.

- Search engines constantly visit sites on the Web to create catalogs of Web pages and keep them up to date.

- Major search engines include: **AltaVista**, **HotBot**, **Open Text**.

Directories

- Search **directories** catalog information by building hierarchical indexes. Since humans assemble the catalogs, information is often more relevant than the indexes that are assembled by Web crawlers. Directories may be better organized than search engine sites, but they will not be as complete or up-to-date as search engines that constantly check for new material on the Internet.

- **Yahoo**, the oldest search service on the World Wide Web, is the best example of Internet search directories. Other major search directories are: **Infoseek**, **Magellan**, **Lycos**.

Multi-Threaded Search Engines

- Another type of search engine, called a **multi-threaded** search engine, searches other Web search sites and gathers the results of these searches for your use.

- Because they search the catalogs of other search sites, multi-threaded search sites do not maintain their own catalogs. These search sites provide more search options than subject-and-keyword search sites, and they typically return more specific information with further precision. However, multi-threaded search sites are much slower to return search results than subject-and-keyword search sites.

- Multi-threaded search sites include **SavvySearch** and **Internet Sleuth**.

■ If you are using Internet Explorer or Netscape Navigator, you can click on the Search button on the toolbar to access a number of search services.

Search Basics

- When you connect to a search site, the home page has a text box for typing the words you want to use in your search. These words are called a **text string**. The text string may be a single word or phrase, or it may be a complex string which uses **operators** to modify the search (see "Search Engines: 21" for more information on operators). Illustrated below is the opening page of Yahoo, one of the oldest and most popular search directories.

Click to initiate search.

Links to Yahoo categories

Access options to refine search.

Regional links

Yahoo! Mail
free email

Shop and Win @ NetBuyer

Win a Sports Dream Trip

Search   options

Yellow Pages - People Search - Maps - Classifieds - Personals - Chat - **Email**
Holiday Shopping - My Yahoo! - News - Sports - Weather - Stoc

- **Arts and Humanities**
  Architecture, Photography, Literature...

- **Business and Economy** [Xtra!]
  Companies, Finance, Employment...

- **Computers and Internet** [Xtra!]
  Internet, WWW, Software, Multimedia...

- **Education**
  Universities, K-12, College Entrance...

- **Entertainment** [Xtra!]
  Cool Links, Movies, Music, Humor...

- **Government**
  Military, Politics [Xtra!], Law, Taxes...

- **Health** [Xtra!]
  Medicine, Drugs, Diseases, Fitness...

- **News and Media** [
  Current Events, Magazines, TV, Newspapers...

- **Recreation and Sports** [Xtra!]
  Sports, Games, Travel, Autos, Outdoors...

- **Reference**
  Libraries, Dictionaries, Phone Numbers...

- **Regional**
  Countries, Regions, U.S. States...

- **Science**
  CS, Biology, Astronomy, Engineering...

- **Social Science**
  Anthropology, Sociology, Economics...

- **Society and Culture**
  People, Environment, Religion...

Yahooligans! for Kids - Beatrice's Guide - MTV/Yahoo! unfURLed - Yahoo! Internet Life
What's New - Weekly Picks - Today's Web Events
Visa Shopping Guide - Yahoo! Store

World Yahoos Australia & NZ - Canada - Denmark - France - Germany - Japan - Korea
Norway - SE Asia - Sweden - UK & Ireland
Yahoo! Metros Atlanta - Austin - Boston - Chicago - Dallas / Fort Worth - Los Angeles
Get Local Miami - Minneapolis / St. Paul - New York - S.F. Bay - Seattle - Wash D.C.

Smart Shopping with **VISA**

How to Suggest a Site - Company Info - Openings at Yahoo! - Contributors - Yahoo! to Go

- Once you have entered a text string, initiate the search by either pressing the Enter key or by clicking on the search button. This button may be called Search, Go Get It, Seek Now, Find, or something similar.
- For the best search results:
  - Always check for misspelled words and typing errors.
  - Use descriptive words and phrases.
  - Use synonyms and variations of words.
  - Find and follow the instructions that the search site suggests for constructing a good search.
  - Eliminate unnecessary words (the, a, an, etc.) from the search string. Concentrate on key words and phrases.
  - Test your search string on several different search sites. Search results from different sites can vary greatly.
  - Explore some of the sites that appear on your initial search and locate terms that would help you refine your search string.

Search Engines: 20

◆ Simple Searches ◆ Refine a Search ◆ Get Help

Simple Searches

■ Searches can be simple or complex, depending on how you design the search string in the text box.

■ A **simple search** uses a text string, usually one or two key words, to search for matches in a search engine's catalog. A simple search is the broadest kind of search.

- The key words may be specific, such as Internet Explorer browser, current stock quotes, or Macintosh computers, or they may be general, such as software, economy, or computer.

- The catalog search will return a list, typically quite large, of Web pages and URLs whose descriptions contain the text string you want to find. Frequently these searches will yield results with completely unrelated items.

■ When you start a search, the Web site searches its catalog for occurrences of your text string. (Some search sites don't have their own catalog, so they search the catalogs of other search sites.) The results of the search, typically a list of Web sites whose descriptions have words that match your text string are displayed in the window of your browser.

■ Each search site has its own criteria for rating the matches of a catalog search and setting the order in which they are displayed.

■ The catalog usually searches for matches of the text string in the URLs of Web sites. It also searches for key words, phrases, and meta-tags (key words that are part of the Web page, but are not displayed in a browser) in the cataloged Web pages.

■ The information displayed on the results page will vary, depending on the search and display options selected and the search site you are using. The most likely matches for your text string appear first in the results list, followed by other likely matches on successive pages.

√ *There may be thousands of matches that contain the search string you specified. The matches are displayed a page at a time. You can view the next page by clicking on the "next page" link provided at the bottom of each search results page.*

- For example, if you do a search on the word *Greek*, you'll get results, as illustrated below, that display links to a wide range of links that have something to do with Greek. Note the number of documents that contain the search word.

  √ *These examples use AltaVista to perform the search. Your results may vary with other search tools.*

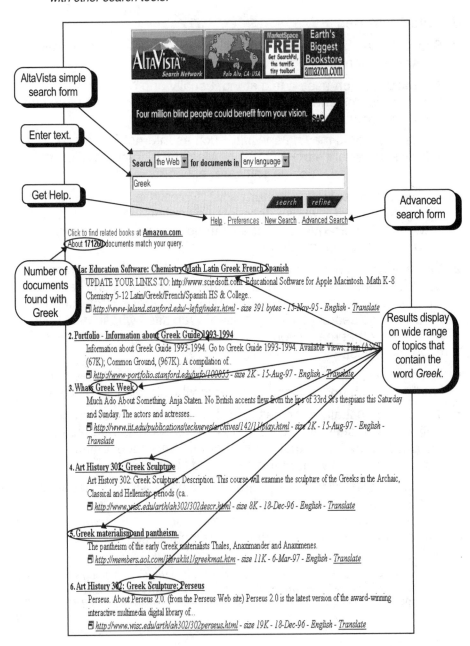

- You can scan the displayed results to see if a site contains the information you are looking for. Site names are clickable links. After visiting a site, you can return to the search site by clicking the Back button on your browser. You can then choose a different site to visit or perform another search.

Refine a Search

- Suppose that you only want to view links that deal with Greek *tragedies*. The natural inclination would be to enter Greek tragedies in the search string to reduce the number of documents that the search tool finds. Note, however, the number of documents that were found when Greek tragedies was entered in this search. Since the search string didn't include a special operator to tell the search engine to look for sites that contain both Greek *and* tragedies, the results display sites that contain Greek *OR* tragedies in addition to sites that contain Greek *AND* tragedies.

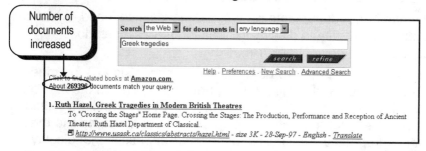

- To reduce the number of documents in this search, enter *Greek* press space once, then enter a plus sign (+) and the word tragedies (Greek +tragedies) then click Search. This tells AltaVista to look for articles that contain Greek *and* tragedies in the documents. Note the results that display when the plus is added to the search.

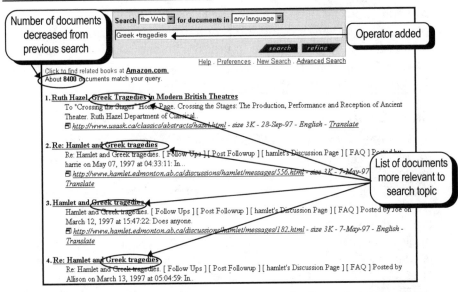

Number of documents decreased from previous search

Search the Web ▾ for documents in any language ▾

Greek +tragedies ◀

Operator added

search refine

Help . Preferences . New Search . Advanced Search

Click to find related books at **Amazon.com.**

About **8400** documents match your query.

1. Ruth Hazel Greek Tragedies in Modern British Theatres
   To "Crossing the Stages" Home Page. Crossing the Stages: The Production, Performance and Reception of Ancient Theater. Ruth Hazel Department of Classical.
   📄 http://www.usask.ca/classics/abstracts/hazel.html - size 3K - 28-Sep-97 - English - Translate

2. Re: Hamlet and Greek tragedies
   Re: Hamlet and Greek tragedies. [Follow Ups] [Post Followup] [hamlet's Discussion Page] [FAQ] Posted by harrie on May 07, 1997 at 04:33:11: In...
   📄 http://www.hamlet.edmonton.ab.ca/discussions/hamlet/messages/556.html - size 3K - 7-May-97 - Translate

   List of documents more relevant to search topic

3. Hamlet and Greek tragedies
   Hamlet and Greek tragedies. [Follow Ups] [Post Followup] [hamlet's Discussion Page] [FAQ] Posted by Joe on March 12, 1997 at 15:47:22: Does anyone.
   📄 http://www.hamlet.edmonton.ab.ca/discussions/hamlet/messages/182.html - size 3K - 7-May-97 - English - Translate

4. Re: Hamlet and Greek tragedies
   Re: Hamlet and Greek tragedies. [Follow Ups] [Post Followup] [hamlet's Discussion Page] [FAQ] Posted by Allison on March 13, 1997 at 05:04:59: In.

- The number of documents listed is dramatically reduced, and the documents displayed display information that is more closely related to the topic, Greek tragedies.

- You can also *exclude* words by using the minus sign (-) to further refine a search and eliminate unwanted documents in the results. For example, if you wanted to find articles about Greek tragedies but not ones that deal with Hamlet, enter a search string like this: *Greek +tragedies -Hamlet*. Note the different results that display:

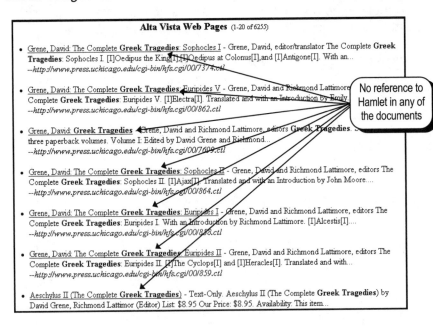

Alta Vista Web Pages (1-20 of 6255)

- Grene, David: The Complete **Greek Tragedies**: Sophocles I - Grene, David, editor/translator The Complete **Greek Tragedies**: Sophocles I. [I]Oedipus the King[I],[I]Oedipus at Colonus[I],and [I]Antigone[I]. With an...
  --http://www.press.uchicago.edu/cgi-bin/hfs.cgi/00/7374.ctl

- Grene, David: The Complete **Greek Tragedies**: Euripides V - Grene, David and Richmond Lattimore Complete **Greek Tragedies**: Euripides V. [I]Electra[I]. Translated and with an Introduction by Emily.
  --http://www.press.uchicago.edu/cgi-bin/hfs.cgi/00/862.ctl

  No reference to Hamlet in any of the documents

- Grene, David: **Greek Tragedies** - Grene, David and Richmond Lattimore, editors **Greek Tragedies**. three paperback volumes. Volume I: Edited by David Grene and Richmond...
  --http://www.press.uchicago.edu/cgi-bin/hfs.cgi/00/7609.ctl

- Grene, David: The Complete **Greek Tragedies**: Sophocles II - Grene, David and Richmond Lattimore, editors The Complete **Greek Tragedies**: Sophocles II. [I]Ajax[I]. Translated and with an Introduction by John Moore....
  --http://www.press.uchicago.edu/cgi-bin/hfs.cgi/00/864.ctl

- Grene, David: The Complete **Greek Tragedies**: Euripides I - Grene, David and Richmond Lattimore, editors The Complete **Greek Tragedies**: Euripides I. With an Introduction by Richmond Lattimore. [I]Alcestis[I]....
  --http://www.press.uchicago.edu/cgi-bin/hfs.cgi/00/858.ctl

- Grene, David: The Complete **Greek Tragedies**: Euripides II - Grene, David and Richmond Lattimore, editors The Complete **Greek Tragedies**: Euripides II. [I]The Cyclops[I] and [I]Heracles[I]. Translated and with...
  --http://www.press.uchicago.edu/cgi-bin/hfs.cgi/00/859.ctl

- Aeschylus II (The Complete **Greek Tragedies**) - Text-Only. Aeschylus II (The Complete **Greek Tragedies**) by David Grene, Richmond Lattimor (Editor) List: $8.95 Our Price: $8.95. Availability: This item...

Get Help

- Check the Help features on the search tool that you are using to see what operators are available. Since there are no standards governing the use of operators, search sites can develop their own. Illustrated on the page 99 are samples of the help available for performing a simple search in AltaVista and Yahoo.

AltaVista Help for Simple Searches

HELP Simple Search

Natural Language queries: (always try this first)

Type a word or phrase or a question (for example, **weather Boston** or **what is the weather in Boston?**), then click Search (or press the Enter key). If the information you want from this sort of query isn't on the first couple of pages, try adding a few more specific words.

Requiring/Excluding Words:

Often you will know a word that will be guaranteed to appear in a document for which you are searching. If this is the case, require that the word appear in all of the results by attaching a "+" to the beginning of the word (for example, to find an article on pet care, you might try the query **dog cat pet +care**). You may also find that when you search on a vague topic, you get a very broad set of results. You can quickly reject results by adding a term that appears often in unwanted articles with a "-" before it (for example, to find a recipe for oatmeal raisin cookies without nuts try **oatmeal raisin cookie -nut* -walnut***).

Exact Phrases:

If you know that a certain phrase will appear on the page you are looking for, put the phrase in quotes. (for example, try entering song lyrics such as **"you ain't nothing but a hound dog"**)

Yahoo Help for Simple Searches

Tips for Better Searching

- **Use Double Quotes Around Words that are Part of a Phrase**

  example `"great barrier reef"` [Search]

- **Specify Words that Must Appear in the Results**
  Attach a + in front words that *must* appear in result documents.

  example: `sting +police` [Search]

- **Specify Words that Should Not Appear in the Results**
  Attach a − in front of words that *must not* appear in result documents.

  example: `python -monty` [Search]

Search Engines: 21

Complex Searches

- When you first connect to a search site, the temptation to type in text and hit the search button is great. Resist it. Taking time to read and understand the search rules of the site will save the time you'll waste by creating a search that yields an overwhelming number of hits. Some of what you want may be buried somewhere in that enormous list, but working your way through the irrelevant sites can waste time, cause frustration, and be very discouraging.

- In "Search Engines: 20," you learned how simply using a plus or minus sign can create a search that gives a more pertinent list of sites. Now, you will see how to use operators to restrict and refine your searches even more.

Operators

- A **complex search** usually contains several words in the text string including **operators** that modify the text string. Operators are words or symbols that modify the search string instead of being part of it.

- Using operators and several descriptive words can narrow your search for information, which means the results will reduce the number of sites that display. This means the resulting list of sites should be more relevant to what you want, thereby saving you time and probably money.

- Each search site develops its own set of restrictions and options to create searches designed to locate specific information. What follows are some of the commonly used operators and how they are used.

Boolean Operators

- **Boolean operators** specify required words, excluded words, and complex combinations of words to be found during a search. Depending on the site, Boolean operators may be represented by words or symbols.

- The most common Boolean operators are:

AND   The documents found in the search must contain *all words* joined by the AND operator. For example, a search for *Microsoft* AND *Internet* AND *Explorer* will find sites which contain all three words (*Microsoft*, *Internet*, and *Explorer*).

OR   The documents found in the search must contain *at least one of the words* joined by the OR operator. The documents may contain both, but this is not required. For example, a search for *Web* OR *Internet* will find sites which contain either the word *Web* or the word *Internet*.

NOT   The documents found in the search must not contain the word following the NOT operator. For example, a search for *Washington* NOT *DC* will find sites which contain the word *Washington* but none about *Washington DC*.

NEAR   The documents found in the search must contain the words joined by the NEAR operator within a specified number of words, typically ten. For example, *RAM* NEAR memory will find sites with the word *RAM* and the word *memory* within ten words of each other.

- Suppose that you can't remember the name of the earthquake that occurred during the World Series in San Francisco in 1989. If you enter relevant words in the simple search function (using the plus sign) in AltaVista, here's what you get:

> Click to find related books at **Amazon.com**
> About **18368** documents match your query.
>
> 1. San Francisco Earthquakes
>   San Francisco Earthquake Links. The Ring of Fire/On Shakey Ground - An Earthquake overview. 1906 Earthquake - Before and After Films. 1906 Earthquake...
>   *http://www.exploratorium.edu/earthquake/sf.earthquakes.html* - size 2K - 11-Oct-95 - English
>
> 2. Why Earthquakes are Inevitable in the San Francisco Bay Area
>   Latest quake info. Hazards & Preparedness. More about earthquakes. Studying Earthquakes. Whats new. Home. Why Earthquakes are Inevitable in the San...
>   *http://quake.wr.usgs.gov/hazprep/BayAreaInsert/inevitable.html* - size 3K - 21-Mar-97 - English
>
> 3. Museums Reach Out With Web Catalogs of Collections /WW November 4 1996
>   Museums Reach Out With Web Catalogs of Collections. By Susan Moran. Earthquakes chase or keep many people away from California. The violent quake of 1989...
>   *http://www.webweek.com/96Nov04/markcomm/arts_sake.html* - size 9K - 17-Apr-97 - English
>
> 4. $A History of California Earthquakes (1 of 101)
>   Content Next. A History of California Earthquakes (Image 1 of 101) Earthquakes in the San Francisco Bay Region. Hayward, 1868. Vacaville, 1892. San...

Results do not answer the question.

- The results display several links to articles about earthquakes in the San Francisco area. If you click on one of these, you may find the earthquake you are looking for.

- Now examine the results of a more complex search using the same words, but using some of the advanced search options available in AltaVista. Entering the search string in the advanced search form of AltaVista displays the following:

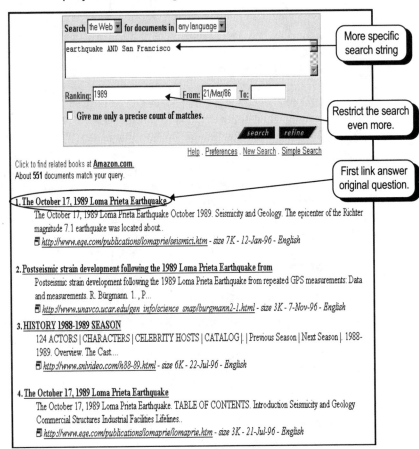

- Use the Advanced search function when you have a specific complex search string; otherwise, use the simple search function. AltaVista will automatically rank the order of the search results when you use the simple search function. When you use the advanced search function, you control the ranking of the results by entering additional search criteria in the Ranking box on the Advanced search form.

Plus (+)/Minus (-) System

- Boolean logic is the basis for the plus and minus system of constructing a search. If the plus/minus sign is not included in the search string, the search engine assumes that you are using OR. That's why when you searched for *Greek tragedies*, AltaVista looked for documents containing either *Greek* or *tragedies*.

Plus sign (+)   Placed immediately in front of a word (no space between the plus sign and the word) means that all documents found must contain that word. (This is similar to the Boolean AND function.) For example, note the results of a search for articles about earthquakes in California, using a search string like this: *earthquakes +California*.

Click to find related books at **Amazon.com**.
About **59247** documents match your query.

1. **$A History of California Earthquakes (5 of 101)**
   Content Previous Next. A History of California Earthquakes (Image 5 of 101) Earthquake damage in San Francisco Bay Region.
   http://www.johnmartin.com/eqshow/cah_0105.htm - size 399 bytes - 5-Dec-96 - English

2. **$A History of California Earthquakes (2 of 101)**
   Content Previous Next. A History of California Earthquakes (Image 2 of 101) State map with major fault systems.
   http://www.johnmartin.com/eqshow/cah_0102.htm - size 389 bytes - 5-Dec-96 - English

3. **Earthquakes in California**
   EARTHQUAKES IN CALIFORNIA. California is the highest earthquake risk area in the contiguous United States. Several large, well-known active faults run...
   http://www.eqe.com/publications/homeprep/eqkesca.htm - size 4K - 26-Nov-95 - English

4. **$A History of California Earthquakes (16 of 101)**
   Content Previous Next. A History of California Earthquakes (Image 16 of 101) Earthquake damage during the 1957 Daly City earthquake.
   http://www.johnmartin.com/eqshow/cah_0116.htm - size 411 bytes - 5-Dec-96 - English

5. **$A History of California Earthquakes (9 of 101)**
   Content Previous Next. A History of California Earthquakes (Image 9 of 101) Earthquake damage during the 1868 Hayward earthquake.
   http://www.johnmartin.com/eqshow/cah_0109.htm - size 407 bytes - 5-Dec-96 - English

---

Minus sign (-)	Place immediately in front of a word (again, no space) means that all documents found will NOT contain that word. (This is the Boolean NOT function.) For example, note the results of search for articles about earthquakes that do *not include* California using a search string like this: *earthquakes -California*.

1. IGS FAQs - Earthquakes
   Q: I was born and raised in South Bend, Indiana and I remember experiencing a tremor on a Fall Saturday, right about mid-day, sometime between 1968 and...
   http://www.indiana.edu/~igs/faqs/faqquake.html - size 3K - 15-Jul-97 - English

2. Index of /ftp/ca.earthquakes/1994/
   Index of /ftp/ca.earthquakes/1994/ Name Last modified Size Description. Parent Directory 30-Jan-94 10:35 - 940106.gif 16-Nov-94 14:18 11K. 940106.ps.Z...
   http://scec.gps.caltech.edu/ftp/ca.earthquakes/1994/ - size 21K - 15-Aug-97 - English

3. Index of /ftp/ca.earthquakes/1993/
   Index of /ftp/ca.earthquakes/1993/ Name Last modified Size Description. Parent Directory 30-Jan-94 10:35 - 930107.ps.Z 08-Aug-94 10:17 40K. 930107.txt.Z...
   http://scec.gps.caltech.edu/ftp/ca.earthquakes/1993/ - size 18K - 15-Aug-97 - English

4. USENET FAQs - sci.geo.earthquakes
   USENET FAQs. sci.geo.earthquakes. FAQs in this newsgroup. Satellite Imagery FAQ - Pointer.
   http://www.cis.ohio-state.edu/hypertext/faq/usenet-faqs/bygroup/sci/geo/earthquakes/top.html - size 328 bytes - 15-Aug-97 - English

5. GEOL 240lxg: Earthquakes
   GEOL 240lxg: Earthquakes. Department: Earth Sciences. Instructor: Sammis, Charles & Teng, Ta-Liang. Semester offered: Fall Spring. Category: Natural...
   http://www.usc.edu/Library/Gede/GEOL240lxg.SammisCharles.html - size 2K - 22-Nov-95 - English

Grouping Operators

- The grouping **operators** join words and phrases together to be treated as a single unit or determine the order in which Boolean operators are applied.

- The most common grouping operators are:

Double quotes	The documents found in the search must contain the words inside double quotes exactly as entered. For example, a search for "*World Wide Web*" will find sites whose descriptions contain the phrase *World Wide Web*, not the individual words separated by other words or the same words uncapitalized.
Parentheses	Words and operators can be grouped to refine searches using parentheses or to define the order in which Boolean operators are applied. For example, a search for (*Internet OR Web*) AND *browser* will find sites whose descriptions contain the words *Internet* and *browser* or *Web* and *browser*. (Note that this is *not* the same search as *Internet* OR *Web AND browser*, which finds sites whose descriptions contain either the word *Internet* or both of the words *Web* and *browser*.)

104

Case Sensitive

- If you enter a word using all lowercase (hamlet), some search engines will look for both upper and lower case versions of the word. If you use uppercase in the search (Hamlet), the search engine will locate documents that only use the uppercase version.

Special Characters and Punctuation

- Special characters and punctuation can also be used to filter results in complex searches. The most widely used character, the asterisk (*) is used when a word in a search can have a number of different forms. Using the asterisk (*) as a wildcard tells the search engine to find documents that contain any form of the word. For example, if you create a search for blue*, note the wide range of documents that show up in the search results.

Click to find related books at **Amazon.com**.
About **800775** documents match your query.

1. Yahoo! - U.S. blue chips slash losses, Nasdaq edges higher
   Yahoo | Write Us | Search | Headlines | Info] [Business - Company - Industry - Finance - PR Newswire - Business Wire - Quotes] Thursday August 14 3:20..
   http://biz.yahoo.com/finance/97/08/14/z0000_21.html - size 4K - 15-Aug-97 - English

2. SI: BLUE DESERT MINING, BDE-ASE
   BLUE DESERT MINING, BDE-ASE. Carlson On-line Profile | Started By: Dale Schwartzenhauer Date: Mar 9 1997 12:52AM EST. Investors should check out BDE, one..
   http://www.techstocks.com/~wsapi/investor/Subject-13562 - size 4K - 15-Aug-97 - English

3. UBL Artist: Daly Planet Blues Band
   Daly Planet Blues Band. The Daly Planet home page The only resource for info on this jam band from Hilton Head Island, SC. Band info, pictures, contact...
   http://www.ubl.com/artists/009821.html - size 6K - 7-Aug-97 - English

4. takuroku blues
   http://www.sainet.or.jp/~akihisa/ - size 242 bytes - 16-Feb-97

5. From Deep Blue to deep space: Take a panoramic look at Mars' surface
   Take a panoramic look at Mars' surface. To view the image* below, you'll need to install IBM's PanoramIX plug-in for the Netscape Navigator browser. The...
   http://www.ibm.com/Stories/1997/07/space6.html - size 2K - 30-Jul-97 - English

- Wildcards are useful if you are looking for a word that could be singular or plural (look for dog*, instead of dog to broaden the search results).

- Other characters that can help limit, filter, and sort results include: %, $, !, | (called the piping symbol), ~ (called the tilde), < (less than), and > (greater than). Check the rules of the individual search engines to see how, or if, these characters can be used.

Major Search Engines and Operators

- Below is a table of the major search tools and how they use some of the search operators. Be sure to check out the search tips and help sections of the sites that you use frequently to see the most current search options. Search tools are constantly updating and improving their sites in response to users' needs.

Search Tool	Boolean operators	+/−	Grouping Operators	Case Sensitivity
AltaVista	✓	✓	✓	✓
AOL NetFind	✓	✓		
Excite	✓	✓	✓	
HotBot	✓	✓	✓	✓
Infoseek		✓	✓	✓
Lycos		✓	✓	
SavvySearch		✓	✓	
Yahoo	✓	✓	✓	✓

Modems and ISPs: Coping with Connecting

Three years ago if you were connecting to the Internet with a modem speed of 14.4 bps you were way ahead of the game. However, current technology—with modem rates as fast as 56.6 bps—allows faster and faster connections.

Now that technology allows us these fast connections, it's frustrating when our modems or poor connections slow us down. This chapter gives you some insight as to why.

1. How does a modem work?

- The word modem is actually an acronym for MOdulator-DEModulator. There are two things you need to know in order to understand how modems work:
  - ♦ All information sent from your computer is considered digital data.
  - ♦ A normal phone line is analog.
- The modem takes the digital information transferred from your computer, converts it to a modulated analog wave or tone so that it can be sent over your phone line. The modem on the other end accepts the analog data and converts it back to digital data so that the target computer can receive the information.

2. I notice that I connect at a different "bps" when logging on to my Internet Service Provider (ISP). Why?

- The acronym "bps" means "bits per second" and refers to the initial speed at which information can be transferred given the presently established modem connection. Although you may not be aware of it, this speed shifts constantly during the course of your connection.
- The speed at which your modem connects is really dependent on the condition of the phone lines in your area and the amount of traffic on your ISP as well as the Internet. *See #4 for more information.*

3. Now that I have a faster modem, do I need a special connection with my ISP to insure that I am connecting at the fastest speed?

- Maybe. There are two 56k modem technologies: Rockwell Corporation's K56flex and 3Com/U.S. Robotics 56k(x2). Check with your ISP to find out which technology they support. Some ISPs support one or the other and some do not support 56k technology at all.

- The modem speed and technology must agree. A K56flex modem must connect to a K56flex modem; likewise, a 56k(x2) must connect to a 56k(x2). You will not get the maximum benefit of a faster modem if your ISP does not support your specific modem technology.

- Once you purchase and install a 56k modem and want to connect to the Internet, there are a couple basic things you should do to ensure optimal performance:

  - Make sure that your ISP supports 56k technology, and, if it does, find out if it supports K56flex or 56k(x2). If the ISP doesn't support 56k technology, you will have to find one that does.

  - ISPs that support 56k modems may have separate phone numbers for connecting to 56k(x2) and K56flex modems. If you are upgrading to a faster modem, you should contact your ISP either online or by phone for more information.

  - If you are connecting to America Online, click on the New Local# option from the pull-down menu on the welcome screen and sign on. Choose a new local number that supports your 56k modem technology.

4. What is phone line noise and how does it affect my modem connection?

- Phone line noise can be caused by any number of things. The main reason is usually old, faulty phone wiring and relay circuits. The reasons can also be:

  - moisture in the phone company's junction boxes

  - electromagnetic frequencies coming from electronic devices near the modem

  - unshielded power lines

  - signals from your local radio station could be coming over your telephone wires

- The quality of your phone lines may be poor due to age and wear and tear. Because of this, the lines are more susceptible to outside and internal interference. This means that everything from crossed lines to radio frequencies may cause static or noise on the line.

- Such noise may not be audible to you, but it definitely interferes with modem connections. Line noise can also cause a modem to loose data during transmission. As a result, when modems connect they do an evaluation of the connection, detecting the amount of noise or the quality of the transmission. If the connection is even slightly corrupted, the modems slow down the rate of transmission thereby minimizing the risk of data loss.

- The path of data sent from your computer over a normal analog phone line from modem to modem is complex. The data must be converted from digital to analog to travel over phone lines. Then it has to be converted back to digital via the target computer's modem. At any point, the data can be corrupted by line noise. As a result, the final conversion is only an approximation of the original digital data sent. Digital phone lines don't have this problem because the connection is cleaner and data conversion is unnecessary.

- To minimize the affects of line noise corruption on the data being transmitted, transmission rates are limited by the FCC. In the best conditions, if you are using a 28.8 or 33.6 modem, the highest rate of transmission is 33.6 bps. If you are using a 56k modem the highest rate of transmission is 53 bps. In most cases transmission and receiving speeds are a lot slower.

5. What is a V.90 modem?

- V.90 is the new, standard protocol set by the International Standards Committee for 56k modems. What this means is that you won't have to worry about which 56k modem to buy because the V.90 will be the standard.

- If you already using a 56k modem, check with the manufacturer to find out about upgrading to the new standard. Once this standard is firmly in place, most of the major manufacturers of 56k modems will tell you how to upgrade your modem without your having to send it back to them.

 ## 6. Should I upgrade my 56k modem to V.90?

- The experts seem to agree that until your ISP upgrades to this protocol leave things as you have them. There are still bugs to work out and ISPs may be slow to adopt the V.90 protocol until it has been tested further.

 ## 7. How can I improve my modem speed?

- If you are connecting at speeds slower than you think your modem should transmit and receive information, in most cases it is not the modem but the phone lines. Until there is a fully digital phone system there is little you can do to speed things up. *See #2 and #4.*

- There are a few simple things you might try:

    ♦ Your ISP may be using a slower modem than you are. Check with your ISP to make sure you are connecting to a modem with a speed comparable to yours.

    ♦ In Windows 95, click the My Computer icon and double-click the Dial-Up connection icon. Select the ISP connection icon and click File, Properties. Click Configure. Make sure that your Maximum speed is set at a speed at least as fast as your modem.

    ♦ You can also edit the Initialization String. Check with your manufacturer or check the modem manual for more information.

- Try plugging your modem into a different phone jack in your house or office and note the connection. There could be a problem with the individual phone jack or connection to the relay box.
- Make sure there are no power cords near your phone line.
- Never use power strips or surge protectors with phone jacks in them. This can cause interference on the phone line.

8. What are typical modem connect speeds?

- Connect speeds depend a great deal on the quality of your phone line. The following are approximate connection speeds under the best line conditions:

Modem	Connection Speed
K56flex	42-46 bps
56k(X2)	44-52 bps
33.6	28.8-33.6 bps
28.8	16.8-28.8 bps
14.4	9600-14.4 bps

- The numbers you see when you connect to your ISP may be lower. Your modem speed is relevant only to the download speed and may well be downloading at a much faster rate than you see posted.

9. What is an ISDN line?

- ISDN is an acronym for Integrated Services Digital Networks.
- It was originally thought that this would be an all fiber-optic connection but it proved too costly to install. Now ISDN works with existing phone lines.
- ISDN lines are capable of speeds from 57.6-128K. This is almost 4 times as fast as some modem connections.
- This service is only offered by a few phone companies, and can be expensive, depending on where you live. Check with your local telephone company for more information.

10. My current ISP doesn't support 56k technology. How do I find a new ISP?

- You can find a new ISP online. Illustrated below is one of the most comprehensive sites for ISPs on the Web.

http//:www.isp.com

ISPs.com — FIND INTERNET SERVICE PROVIDERS *FAST!*

Looking For An Internet Service Provider?

Find the best deal from our database of over 4,000 ISPs.

Other Searches:

Search By Price

Search By Name

National ISPs

Toll-Free ISPs

Search By Area Code

Enter your telephone area code to find all the Internet Service Providers in your area.

Area Code: ☐

Search

Other Resources:

- Tips & Tricks for the Web
- Shareware for the

11. I am considering changing my ISP. Are there any specific things I should ask a potential service provider?

- There are a few things that you should find out about the ISP's service:

  - Ask if their modem line would be a local call for you or see if they have a modem line with an 800-phone number.

  - Be sure to ask if there is a flat charge for unlimited service or if you are billed by the time you spend online.

  - See if the service agreement is on a month-by-month basis or if you need to sign up for larger blocks of time. Some ISPs offer discount prices if you pay in advance for semi-annual or annual service.

  - Check if the ISP's modem speed to which you're connecting is at least as fast as your modem.

  - Find out what the user-to-modem ratio is. The fewer people connecting to a modem the better.

  - Many IPS's charge a setup or activation fee, but others don't. You may want to shop around to find one that doesn't charge.

  - Ask about their anti-spamming policies. *See Spam: The New Junk Mail.* Many ISPs are more actively involved with spam control.

  - Some ISP's (such as AOL) provide free Web space so that you can post your own Web page. If this is something that you would be interested in, be sure to ask.

Downloads: The Lost Files

If you're like most people, you download or retrieve files and e-mail attachments and save them on your computer for future access. In a sense, you're creating a personal Internet library. As you begin your file library, you should learn the different file types and the programs necessary to open them. This section will give you information on the possible problems you may encounter when downloading files and simple ways to organize these files so that you know where they are on your computer at all times.

12. What is "downloading?"

- Downloading a file or an e-mail attachment is the act of transferring a file or an e-mail attachment from another computer or your mail server to your computer.

- A download is the actual file that is transferred to your computer.

13. When I download a file or program, I get a prompt asking if I want to save it to a disk or open it directly to my computer. Is one way better than the other?

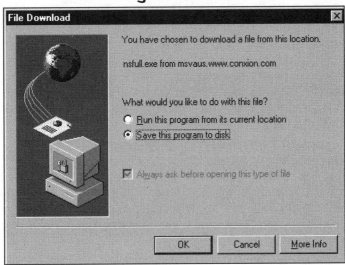

- When downloading files you may receive a prompt similar to the one pictured above. Most people save downloads directly to their hard drive rather than to a disk simply because it is easier. Most Internet experts suggest downloading files—especially program files—to a disk rather than directly to your hard drive in case the file contains a virus. *See Viruses: Computer Bugs.* However, if you are absolutely sure the file or program is virus-free, saving it directly to your hard drive is fine.

- There are two important advantages to saving a file to a disk. First, saving it to a disk allows you to check the file for harmful computer viruses with a virus scanner or antivirus program. One of several fairly inexpensive antivirus shareware programs can be downloaded from the Tucows software site: *http://www.tucows.com.* Search for Antivirus under the heading software Utilities.

- Second, storing a file on a disk allows you to view the file without storing it on your computer, thereby saving precious hard disk space. Some files, however, are too large to save to disk.

14. Sometimes I download a multimedia file and can't open it. This has happened with Internet Explorer, Netscape and AOL. Why can I open some and not others?

- In many cases the reason that you cannot open a downloaded multimedia file or e-mail attachment is that you probably don't have the necessary application needed to open the file. *See #19.*

- **Netscape and Explorer** include software programs called **plug-ins**, which work in conjunction with the browser and support the most-common multimedia file types. The plug-ins open multimedia files in the browser window. You may not even be aware that these separate software programs exist because they run behind the scenes.

- If you download a file and the plug-in required to open the file is not part of your browser program, a prompt should display with a link to an area where you can download one of several plug-ins. Downloading one of these plug-ins should enable you to open the file. Once you install the necessary plug-in, it should work with your browser and open any future files of the same type. *See #19.*

- **America Online** supports some audio and graphic formats but does not have the same plug-in support found with Explorer or Netscape. You need separate plug-ins to view some multimedia files. Go to **Keyword: Multimedia Experience** for a list of popular plug-in programs and information on the file types they support.

- You can download the most popular shareware plug-in programs at the Tucows (*tucows.com*) Web site.

15. I am able to open most of the e-mail attachments I receive. However, I just got one that is an .exe file and I can't open it. What should I do?

- Executable files or program files can be identified by their .exe extension. *See #19 for more information on file types.* These files are sometimes self-extracting programs and will run simply by double-clicking on the file. In other cases you will have to install the file before you can run it.

16. On AOL I sometimes get an error message that the file is too large for AOL to open. I never see this message on Netscape or Internet Explorer. What does it mean?

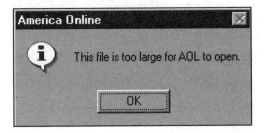

- If AOL can't open the file, the error message seen above will display. In most cases you will get this message because AOL cannot open multi-file e-mail attachments and the file will most likely be labeled a .MIM file because of the encoding used to send it. *See #17 below.*
- Sometimes the file is too large for the server to handle.

17. What is a MIME file?

- MIME or Multipurpose Internet Mail Extensions is not really a file type but rather a standardized encoding method used to send non-text (binary) files via e-mail. Files that are not plain text files such as multimedia, spreadsheet, word processing files (files with software application formatting), graphics, etc., are called binary files and have to be encoded, or translated, into a language computers can understand in order to be sent electronically. MIME encoding is one of the ways this is done.
- MIME files have a .mme or .mim extension because the mail server could not decode the file before downloading it. The file has not been translated or decoded back into its original state. If you open a MIME file you will see a series of letters and symbols. What you are seeing is the encoding language used to send the file electronically. The file must be decoded before it can be seen or heard.
- If your e-mail server is MIME-compliant, it will decode the MIME encoded file and return it back to its original state before you download it to your computer. The extension you see is the extension of the actual file type. Remember, a .mim extension only means that the file wasn't decoded and that it is some sort of binary file.
- MIME encoding and decoding is done without any assistance from you.
- There may be times when your mail server will not be able to decode the MIME-encoded file sent to you. In this instance you will need a decoder application, which you can get from any software site. But before you do, try using a zip application to open the file. *See Compressed Files: Zip It!* In many cases MIME files are just multi-file attachments that, once opened, can be viewed by applications already contained on your computer.

18. What do I need to know about opening a .zip file?

- A zip file is a series of files compressed into one file or a large file compressed into a much smaller file. Zipped files are much smaller files and can be downloaded and uploaded faster and stored more easily. *See Compressed Files: Zip It!*

- A zip file has to be decompressed or restored to its original size to be viewed.

- **America Online** will decompress downloaded zip files that you receive as e-mail attachments at sign-off. If AOL is not automatically unzipping files, you will need to go to the Download Preferences area.

  To set file decompression options for AOL:

  ◆ Click **Members**, **Preferences**.

  ◆ Click [Download].

  ◆ Select download preferences.

  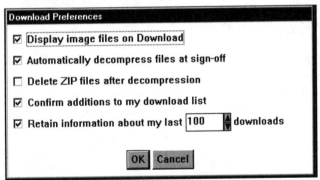

  ◆ Click [OK].

- **Internet Explorer and Netscape** require a zip program like WinZip to unzip files. This shareware program is easy to use. *See Compressed Files: Zip It!* The WinZip program can automatically open and unzip the file so that you can view its contents.

19. What are file extensions?

- A file extension is the three or four letters that appear after the file name. For example: boxer.jpg. The file name is boxer and the extension .jpg tells you the file type.

- Knowing the type of file you are trying to open will tell you the application needed to open the file.

- Following is a list of the most common file types, their extensions, and suggested software applications recommended by the ZDNet Software Library Web site experts. Though you may be able to work with these files directly through your browser, the suggested software may offer additional features.

- **au**
  Internet sound file. Any audio application should play this file. You may download Jet-Audio from the ZDNet site and try it free of charge. If you wish to keep it, you must pay $29.00 for the application.

- **avi**
  Windows video format. Windows 95 has built-in viewing capabilities. Netscape and Explorer support these files. The AviLxp program available from the ZDNet site comes highly recommended. If you decide to keep it, the cost is $25.00.

- **exe**
  An executable program or a self-extracting file. Such files often need to be installed before they can be viewed.

- **gif**
  A graphics file. Can be viewed with any viewer. WWW Gif Animator allows you to do all sorts of things with your gif files, such as manipulate and edit them. Price: $20.00.

- **html, htm**
  HTML or Hypertext Markup Language is the standardized code in which Web pages are written. **CoolCat** is a Web page creation program that is free to try, but not so cheap to keep, at $99.00. Highly recommended by the experts at ZDNet.

- **jpg, jpeg**
  A very common graphic file format. Almost any graphics viewer will open these files. Try **Lview Pro**.

- **mid, midi**
  MIDI format music files. Netscape, Explorer, and AOL support these file types. Windows 95 Media Player also supports these files. **MidiPlus** is highly rated by the ZDNet site and is free.

- **mov**
  QuickTime video format. Many Windows applications support these files. ZDNet recommends **Juke Vox**, which is free.

- **mpg, mpeg**
  Moving Pictures Experts Group digital video file. These files may be difficult to open unless you have a program like **Amaplay**. The program is free to try, but $10.00 if you decide to keep it.

- **pdf**
  Adobe Acrobat Portable Document Format files. You will need the **Adobe Acrobat Reader** to open these file types. The Adobe Reader software is free.

- **sit**
  A Mac zip file. Mac compressed files are called Stuffit Archives. **WinPack32 Deluxe v2.2** says they are able to decompress any compressed file. This program costs $21.00.

- **txt**
  A generic text file that contains no formatting. Can be opened with any text reader or word processing program.

- **tiff, tif**
  A large, high quality image format file. **AI Picture Utility** supports most image files and has a full compliment of editing features. Price: $29.95.

- **wav**
  A Windows sound file. Windows audio program supports these files comfortably so you don't need a special application to open them.

- **zip**
  A file compression format. Use **PKZip** or **WinZip** programs to open these files. Both programs are free to try and $49.00 to keep.

20. Sometimes I download a file and have no idea where to find it on my computer. What can I do?

- **America Online** automatically sends all downloads to the AOL download folder unless you specify otherwise. This folder is located as a sub-folder of the AOL program.

- To find out where a downloaded file is located when using AOL:

  - ♦ Click **File**, **Download Manager**.

  - ♦ Click [Show Files Downloaded].

  - ♦ Click on the file in question from the Files You've Downloaded list.

  - ♦ Click [Show Status].

- The file information box displays with the drive, directory, folder, and file name.

- You don't have to be online to do the above procedure.

- Before you start downloading files from the Web using **Netscape** or **Explorer**, first choose the drive and the directory where you want to store downloaded files. Create a new folder with a name like "NetscapeDownloads" or "ExplorerFiles" where you can store all your saved files.

122

- When you start to save a file from the Web, a Save As dialog box opens—this dialog box has the same options that you would see in a word processor's Save As dialog box.

- From the Save in drop-down list select the drive and folder in which you want to save the file.

- Once you save your first downloaded file to the new folder, that folder will become your browser's default folder each time you want to save something. Then, you will always know where to find downloaded files. *See Windows: Just the Basics.*

Spam: The New Junk Mail

http://www.spam.abuse.net/spam/

 Promote Responsible Net Commerce:
Help Stamp Out Spam!

Before the advent of Usenets (*see Usenet: The People's Forum*) and e-mail, **spam** used to refer to canned luncheon meat. These days spam is Unsolicited Commercial E-Mail (UCE) or junk e-mail. Spam has made a lot of people very angry.

If you have an e-mail address, you have probably received spam. If you haven't, you will soon enough. The amount of junk e-mail being sent over the Internet is growing at an alarming rate.

As the amount of spam grows, so do the complaints from innocent e-mail users who are tired of being harassed with get-rich-quick scams, porn site ads, or other unsavory and unscrupulous offers.

Many Internet Service Providers are taking action against spammers. Some, like America Online and Reply.net, have even taken legal action against spammers.

http://www.reply.net

Around the world in seconds ^{tm}

ReplyNet

Generally, ISPs simply cancel a spammer's account. Unfortunately, some spammers now send e-mail with bogus return addresses or use trial e-mail services that expire or that they cancel before any action can be taken against them.

21. What is spam?

- Originally, spam entered Internet lingo as a term meaning to post numerous messages to one or many Internet newsgroups (Usenets). Spam now also refers to unsolicited, unwanted e-mail. The content of the spam is irrelevant.

22. How does my e-mail address get on a junk e-mail list?

- You get junk e-mail in much the same way you get junk snail mail (mail delivered by the post office). Your name somehow gets on a list that is then sold to an agency that compiles addresses based on consumer or Internet interest. These lists are bought by spammers.

- Spammers also comb newsgroup postings for e-mail addresses to add to their list.

- Your e-mail address can be recovered when you connect to a Web site server. When you make a connection, it is possible for the target server to use a tool that can retrieve your e-mail address. Your e-mail address is then added to a growing list of people who, based on your interest in that particular site, have similar tastes. Then the spamming begins.

23. To whom do I complain about spam?

- If you reply to the message and ask to be removed from their list, the mail may be returned to you as undeliverable or your response may generate a new solicitation. Although sending a request to be removed from a spam list may be successful, as a general rule of thumb, **do not reply directly to the solicitation**.

- Sending a nasty message or seeking revenge through mail bombing (sending an outrageous amount of mail to the sender) may result in your service provider closing *your* account.

- According to the Public Access Networks Corporation at *Panix.com*, one way to combat unwanted e-mail is to send the message to the postmaster at the offending site. Forward the message as you would any other but replace the name in the e-mail address with *postmaster* leaving the domain information the same.

- For example: if you receive spam from *calvinxxx@spammer.com*, first copy the address of the sender so that you can insert it into the Forward address field.

- Delete the name *calvinxxx* and add *postmaster*. Leave the domain name—everything after the @ symbol—the same. Then compose a request asking to be removed from the list. Be civil as the postmaster isn't to blame.

- On the following page is the response from *postmaster@Netcom.com* to a spam complaint:

> Hello,
>
> Your mail has been forwarded to our Security Department (formerly known as Abuse). In the future, to ensure the most expedient reply, please direct any reports of abuse from NETCOM customers to:
>
> **abuse@netcom.com**
>
> Please be sure to examine the headers of the messages that you receive and make sure that they are indeed NETCOM users. Note: If the messages are not from a NETCOM user, please report them to the postmaster or administrator of the sender, by mailing to:
>
> **postmaster@domain**
>
> where domain is the domain of the user sending the e-mail. If you have any other questions or concerns, please do not hesitate to contact us again.
>
> Andy

- Most ISPs now have an address dedicated to handling spam complaints. Check with your ISP or your e-mail service for more information.

24. How do Netscape, Internet Explorer, and AOL handle Spam?

- **Netscape** and **Internet Explorer** are not Internet Service Providers—they are Web browsers—and therefore do not directly handle spam. Your ISP houses your e-mail server. Contact your ISP for more information on handling spam.

- **America Online** handles spam at screen name TOSSpam. They ask that you *forward* the original e-mail—do not copy and paste it into a new e-mail form.

25. AOL's tips on stopping junk mail:

- America Online offers these valuable tips on dealing with junk mail:

  ◆ **Do not respond to junk e-mail**. It only confirms that your e-mail address is correct and that you've read the message.

  ◆ Most junk e-mail addresses are fake. In AOL you can block the name and/or domain. Go to keyword: **mail controls** for more information.

  ◆ If the advertiser lists a phone number, call and complain. This may be an effective way of taking you off the list.

  ◆ Report unwanted junk mail to your ISP. Making noise can help win the battle against receiving junk mail.

26. Why would an ISP care about spammers? Is spamming illegal?

- Some spam is illegal. Pyramid schemes—which are similar to chain letters—are illegal as well as some forms of pornography.

- An incredible amount of spam traffic clogs mail server networks. Systems administrators have to spend time and money to clean up the undelivered mail and respond to spam complaints. If an ISP does nothing to stop spamming, their customers may view them as disreputable and switch servers. Therefore, it is in the ISP's best interest to take an active part in stopping spam.

27. What are Anti-spam software programs and are they any good?

- E-mail anti-spam programs like **Spam Exterminator** allows you to control the e-mail you receive. These programs not only delete e-mail from the mail server based on criteria you decide, but they can also delete e-mail with Spam indicators in the subject or address fields.

- Spam Exterminator keeps a running list of spammers. As of May, 1998 the list totals over 16,000.

- You can set up very specialized criteria for detecting spam such as headings that include "HUGE OPPORTUNITY" or other common spam subject headings. Once you set the criteria, a program like Spam Exterminator does the rest.

- Be careful when using these programs. Read the particulars carefully; these programs can also delete e-mail you may want to read.

- You can download an anti-spam shareware program from the *hotfiles.ZDNet.com* software site. Type *spam* in the search box to view anti-spam software programs.

28. Do anti-spam shareware programs work with America Online?

- No. You must have a POP (Post Office Protocol) address in order to use these programs. E-mail is an AOL feature and does not have a separate e-mail server that requires a POP address.

- AOL has built-in mail filters to control unwanted mail. You can set these controls by going to Keyword: Mail Controls and choose the settings that makes sense for you and your family.

To set Mail Controls:

◆ You must be signed on to the Master Account. This is the name to which the bill is sent.

◆ Go to keyword: **mail controls**.

◆ Click **SET UP MAIL CONTROLS**.

√ *A screen will appear that displays all of the screen names on your account.*

◆ Select the screen name for which you'd like to use Mail Controls.

◆ Click **Edit**.

√ *A screen will display, allowing you to select Mail Controls settings for the screen name that you have selected.*

◆ Select from the mail control options listed.

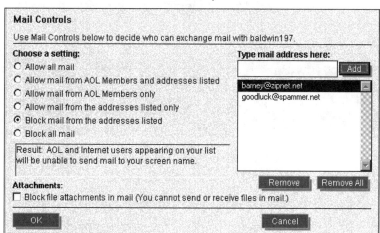

◆ Click **OK**.

29. Where can I go to find more information about spam?

Fight Spam on the Internet!

Boycott Internet Spam!

http://spam.abuse.net/

♦ See Frequently Asked Questions to find out more information on spam, as well as suggestions on how to market on the Internet.

http://www.cauce.org/

♦ CAUCE is a group of Internet users who have joined together to introduce and promote legislation to make spam illegal.

ANTI-SPAM CAMPAIGN!

Directory of Spam-Fighting Information and Resources

http://www.ao.net/waytosuccess/newbie.html

♦ This site contains hundreds of facts concerning spam including anti-spam government and legal resources, ISP acceptable use policies, solutions to stop spam, and much more.

Web Searches:
The Needle in the Haystack

Most people find Web searches frustrating. The reasons range from "I don't know how to search the Web" to "Every time I attempt a search I get thousands of results—but nothing that I'm searching for!"

The Web has millions of pages of information and there is no sure-fire way to return the results you seek. There are, however, a few basic tips that will almost always help you find what you want. It's the old needle in the haystack. If you are patient and methodical in your search, you can find almost anything on the Web.

Following are six search tips for three of the most popular search sites. Each search site is different but some search techniques are universal.

Explore each site using the information in this section. You'll be surprised at how little time it will take you to start searching effectively.

Basic sections 19-21 in the front of this book give you more information on simple searches, complex searches, Boolean operators, special characters, and punctuation.

 ## 30. AltaVista:

http://altavista.digital.com/

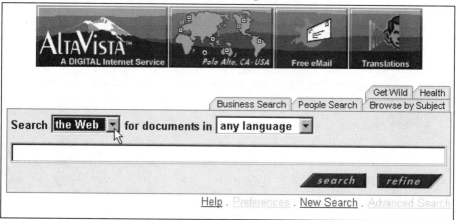

- Input the most important words (the keywords) of your search in the Search box. Make sure all words are spelled correctly.
    - Enter the keywords of your query into the search box.
    - For example: If you are searching the Web because you are studying medieval music, you might enter the keywords *medieval music study* into the search box. This will return pages with the words medieval, medieval studies, the study of medieval music, etc.
    - If what you really want is information on medieval music and not general medieval studies, you'll need to modify the information you typed into the Search box.
- You may need to modify the search information you entered into the search box in order to narrow the search results. This will help you find more information specifically relevant to your search.
    - To modify your search string *medieval study music*, put a (+) sign in front of the word *music* and a (−) sign in front of the word *study*. This will return pages that contain both *medieval* and *music* but not the word *study*.
    - If you are actually interested in finding information on the study of medieval music, you might try entering *medieval studies +music*. There is no space between the (+) sign and the word. There is a space between the words. This search should return pages on the study of medieval music.
- Always use lowercase letters when searching the Web using AltaVista unless you are using proper nouns.
    - When entering keywords, use all lowercase letters. This method will return pages where the keywords are displayed in both lowercase and initial capitalization.
    - Capitalize your keywords if they are proper nouns such as names (the speeches of President Clinton) or places (Taj Mahal Palace). Using uppercase will return Web sites and pages where the keywords appear only in uppercase.
- You can also enter exact phrases into the search text box.
    - If you are looking for pages that contain an exact quote or phrase like a song lyric, enclose the phrase in the Search box with quotation marks.
    - For example: To find a copy of Dr. Martin Luther King's "I Have a Dream" speech, enter the words *"I Have a Dream"* in quotation marks in the Search box. You can narrow this search even further by adding *+Dr. Martin Luther King*.

- ♦ You can also do a search by telephone number. Any information contained on a Web page is valid keyword information. For example, entering 800-528-3897 will return pages from the DDC Publishing Web site.

- • Search Usenets (Newsgroups) to read public opinion and postings on thousands of topics.

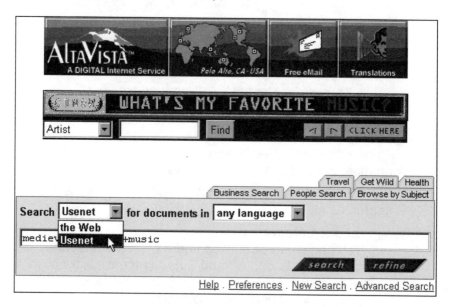

- ♦ You may be surprised at the amount and variety of Usenet (Newsgroup) postings available and on thousands of interests and topics. Entering the search on *Medieval –study +music* into the Search box and clicking Usenet from the Search pull-down menu, returned links to recordings of medieval music, graphic files of medieval musicians, even links to a pinball game that incorporates medieval music.

- • Go to the AltaVista search areas found at the top of the search box to search a collection of Web pages and sites on everything from Travel to People.

- ♦ Go to specialized search areas to get information on topics from travel to health by clicking the category tabs located at the top of the search box. These areas contain Web sites and pages specific to the tab topic.

- ♦ Click on AltaVista Help to get more information on searches.

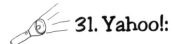 ## 31. Yahoo!:

http://www.Yahoo!.com

- Yahoo! search results' screen can be difficult to understand. That's why it's good to learn how Yahoo! searches for information and displays search results.

  ♦ Yahoo! searches the four databases contained in its search catalog.

    * **Yahoo! Categories:**
      Web pages are organized under different categories like History, Economy, and Entertainment. Clicking on the Category link will take you to an area where results are organized under sub-categories.

    * **Yahoo! Web Sites:**
      This area contains a list of Web page links that are relevant to your search. If Yahoo! contains no information in its catalog, it will search the AltaVista catalog.

    * **Yahoo!'s Net Events & Chat:**
      Clicking this link will take you to a list of events and live chats on the Web that are relevant based on words in your search string.

    * **Most Recent News Articles:**
      Yahoo! will search a database of over 300 online publications for articles that contain your keywords.

  ♦ You can do a general Web search by clicking the Yahoo! option below the search box. To search for information from Usenet (newsgroups) or for a person's e-mail address, click on the appropriate option.

- Yahoo! prioritizes and displays search results in three ways:
  - ◆ Search results are prioritized and listed under three categories:
    - ∗ Documents with the most matches to your keywords
    - ∗ Document titles with the most matching keywords
    - ∗ Categories that contain the most general information based on your keywords
- Enter the keywords of your search in the search box. Make sure the words are spelled correctly.
  - ◆ Be as specific as possible when entering keywords into the search box.
  - ◆ Use a **(+)** sign in front of any keyword that must appear in the document and a minus **(-)** sign in front of words that should not. For example: If you are searching for information on *peanut farming* your search might return many pages on peanut butter. If this happens, add *butter* to the search box and put a minus sign **(-)** in front of it. The results should return pages on *peanut farming* and no information about *peanut butter.*
- Yahoo! provides search syntax options to help you modify your search.
  - ◆ To display search syntax options, click the *options* link next to the Search button from the home page.

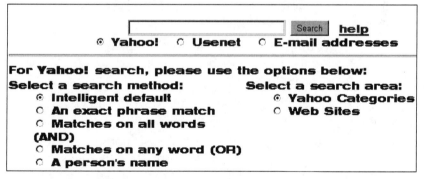

  - ◆ Enter your keywords in the text box.
  - ◆ Choose from the list of options:
    - ∗ **Intelligent default:**
      This is a typical Yahoo! search. Select either to search Yahoo! categories or to search for Web sites that contain pages relevant to your keywords.

* **An exact phrase match:**
  Allows you to search for an exact phrase match based on your keywords.

* **Matches on all words (AND):**
  Returns pages or Web sites that contain all the words you've entered into the Search box.

* **Matches on any words (OR):**
  Returns pages or Web sites that contain any of your keywords. This category will yield the greatest number of returns.

* **A person's name:**
  Returns pages with a person's name that matches your keywords.

- You can also do a search by document title and URL.

  - Search the Yahoo! catalog to return search results with your keywords either in the title of the document page or in the URL (Web address).

    * Place a *t:* in front of one or more keywords to yield Web pages with the keywords in the title of the page.

    * For example: to search for Web pages on the television show *Seinfeld* enter *t:Seinfeld*.

    * Place a *u:* in front of keywords to yield returns with the keyword in the URL. Your search should return pages dedicated to the subject of your keywords.

    * For example: to search for Web pages dedicated to everything regarding *Seinfeld*—including the TV show— enter *u:Seinfeld*.

- Yahoo! has specialized areas where you can search for everything from weather to online shopping sites.

  - Click on any of the links on the Yahoo! home page to search for anything from stock quote information to buying a pet or an automobile. These links contain extensive information.

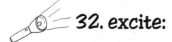 **32. excite:**

http://www.excite.com/

- Enter concepts and ideas rather than keywords into the search box.

  - excite searches the Web by concept using Intelligent Concept Extraction (ICE) to find the relationships between words and ideas.

  - Using ICE, excite begins looking for pages and sites with information relevant to your keywords. Although you can enter phrases and questions, it is still important to choose your keywords carefully.

  - For example: instead of searching for information on *mad cow disease*, you may be more interested in *the effects of mad cow disease on humans*. You can enter this whole statement in the search box. Instead of getting pages that contain one or the other word, excite returns pages that discuss the effects of mad cow disease on humans.

- You can further modify your search by adding words supplied by excite based on the keywords or phrase you've entered.

- After your initial search, the excite Search Wizard suggests relevant words that you might add to your search to narrow the results. Click on any of the words to add them to the search box. You can delete the word from the search box by deselecting it. Click the Search Again button to begin a new search.
- Choosing one or more of excite's suggested words will enable excite to return pages highly relevant to your search.
- excite sorts search results by relevance. excite displays the closest matches at the top of the results page. There is also a percentage rating next to each listing indicating the degree of relevance based on the number of your keywords the page contains.

- Click the *More Like This* link next to the URL to see pages similar to the one displayed.
  - Each page also has a *More Like This* link next to the URL just below the summary. Clicking on this link will return pages similar to the result page you selected.

- Modify the words in your search phrase by using the (+) and (–) signs.
  - Use a (+) sign in front of words that are essential to the information you're looking for and a (–) in front of words that should not be included in the results pages. Do not put a space between the symbol and the word. Do add a space between words and words with symbols.

- You can activate a "Power Search." This search uses the excite Search Wizard to help focus your search.
  - The excite Search wizard helps you prioritize your keywords so that the results more closely match what you you're trying to find.
  - Power Search performs an advanced search without advanced syntax characters or Boolean operators. *See the Search Basics sections 19-21 for more information.*
  - Click on the Power Search link located to the left of the search box on the excite home page. Enter the keywords or idea into the search box.

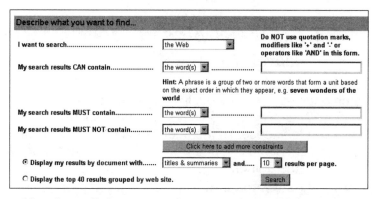

- ◆ Use the pull-down menus to search the Web, newsgroups, or excite sites around the world.

- ◆ Enter the words from your search that can be included in your search results.

- ◆ Enter the words that must be contained in the results.

- ◆ Enter words that must not be contained based on the search results you've gathered so far. If, for example you are looking for information on *peanut farming* but some of your returns contain information on *peanut butter*, enter the word *butter* in this box.

- ◆ You can choose to display search results by title only and by how many results you want to view per page.

- ◆ You can also choose to display the top 40 results grouped by Web site.

- Your search should always contain more than one word.

- ◆ Entering only one word into the search text box will return millions of pages containing that word.

- ◆ Enter as many relevant words—within reason—as you can. With excite, you can use numerous features to sort through this list and ultimately find exactly what you desire.

- ◆ Click the Help button to read more on excite search.

33. Are there software programs that search the Web?

- There are several shareware programs that will search several search engines simultaneously based on your keywords. The ZDNet *hotfiles.com* site has several search shareware programs from which to choose. Remember this is not free software. If you decide to continue using shareware after the trial period, you have to pay the author.

  - **Hurricane WebSearch** is a shareware program from Gate Comm and got the highest rating from the ZDNet software library (*http//: www.hotfiles.ZDNet.com*). This software can conduct searches in "lightning-fast time." You set criteria such as the number of results you want to retrieve from each site and the maximum waiting time for gathering information and Hurricane WebSearch does the rest. Free to try. $14.95 to keep.

  - **WebSeeker** searches over 100 search engines like Yahoo!, Lycos, and Webcrawler to locate information. This type of search engine is called a meta-searcher because it simultaneously searches many search engines at once. WebSeeker creates individual keyword searches for each search engine, displays the results, sorts them, removes duplicates, collates, and then presents the results. WebSeeker can help you manage your results by classifying each search result. Free to try. $49.95 to keep.

URL Troubleshooting: Addressee Unknown

Web sites change or go out of business every day. Files are located on Web servers all over the world and sometimes the location of these files change. It can be frustrating to access information one day, but the next day find that the file is not available or the site has moved with no forwarding address.

Here are a few tips and answers to troubleshooting questions.

34. What is a URL?

- URL stands for Uniform Resource locator or, in short, the Web address. It is a locator command used within the World Wide Web system to create or hunt for linked sites. *See page 7 for more information on URLs.*

35. I visited a Web site yesterday and had no trouble. Today I got an odd error message "404 Not Found." What happened?

- There are several things that may have happened. The file name may have changed, the server name may have changed, or you may have typed a spelling error in the URL.

- In many cases it's just a matter of trying the address again. There may be a great deal of Web traffic to the Web site or congestion on your browser server. Try the same address a couple times.

36. Check the URL you have entered carefully.

- It's very easy to type one wrong letter or symbol. This may not seem like a big deal but, in fact, it may be the reason you can't connect to the site you want.

- URLs—especially the long complex addresses—must be typed exactly. That includes correct spelling and punctuation.

- In addition, pay attention to how upper- and lowercase letters are used in the URL. Sometimes computer servers are case-sensitive and will not understand a name entered in lowercase when it should be capitalized.

37. Is it possible that the file has moved but the server address is the same?

- Absolutely. A server houses many files and it is possible for files to get shifted around.

- The first thing you might do is to shorten the address. Take the Web address and work backwards deleting the last entry of the URL first. For example:

    ◆ I'm looking for tax sites on the Tax Resources Web site. The address is:
    http://www2.best.com/~ftmexpat/html/taxesites.html

    ◆ It is possible that the tax site information has been placed somewhere else on the *best.com* server and that the tax site information is being housed somewhere else.

    ◆ Delete the *taxsites.html.* That will take you to a higher directory on the Web page where you may find information on where the file has moved.

    ◆ Continue to work your way backward through the address until you find what you're looking for or until you are convinced that the file no longer exists.

38. What is a DNS error?

- DNS is an acronym for Domain Name Service. In short, the URLs you see actually have number codes called IP (Internet Protocol) addresses.

- An IP address consists of four sets of numbers ranging from 0 to 255. Computers only understand codes and each host computer on the Internet has a number code. However, http protocol allows us to enter in the name of the site instead of its corresponding number.

- If you watch the Status bar of your browser as you connect to a Web site, sometimes you will see the IP address entered as the computers connect.

- Once you enter the URL, the DNS finds the matching number code or IP address and makes a connection. If the DNS is unable to find an IP address match, you will get a DNS error. Check the URL information you've entered and try again.

39. Use Search Engines.

- This may be your only way to find out where a Web page has actually moved. *See #30-33 for more information on searches.*

- Enter keywords about the Web page using one of the search sites like Yahoo!, Infoseek, or AltaVista and see what comes back. There is a chance that you will find that the Web page you are looking for on another site. The worst thing that can happen is that you get the information you need from another site source.

Usenet: The People's Forum

Usenet is a forum for exchanging ideas, viewpoints, and information with people all over the world. Some would argue that Usenet is even more popular than e-mail. The great thing about Usenet is that instead of communicating with one person at a time, you are communicating with potentially millions of people.

 ## 40. What is Usenet?

- Usenet stands for "Users Network." Usenet is a separate system independent of the Internet and you must use a separate news server to log on. However, you can access Usenet using the Internet. The Usenet system exists to house newsgroups and newsgroups' files.

- Newsgroups are like huge message boards where you can find information on everything from technical and scientific topics to politics, pastimes, and gossip. New newsgroups are added every day. There are over 13,000 newsgroups from all over the world on Usenet. Generally, when you use the term Usenet you are discussing newsgroups. However, the terms are frequently used interchangeably.

- Using Usenet you can access newsgroups to ask a question, post an opinion or idea on a particular topic, or share binary files (*see #55*) relevant to the newsgroup focus with thousands of people.

- Once you find a newsgroup whose focus interests you, you can find articles (called postings) from experts willing to share their knowledge with anyone with similar interests. You can also ask questions of subscribers to the newsgroup and usually get help.

- The exchange of information is what makes Usenet so popular. When you find a newsgroup with articles of interest to you, subscribe to the newsgroup. Each time you connect to your news server, the server will download articles posted to each group in your personal subscription list.

41. How do I access Usenet?

- Most ISP's provide access to Usenet through a news server. You will have to configure your browser or Internet program so that it will know the location of your ISP news server. You do this in the same way you configured the browser to find your ISP mail server.

- Below you will find a list of browsers and their corresponding newsgroups:

    ◆ Netscape Communicator: **Netscape Collabra**

    ◆ Internet Explorer: **Outlook Express**

    ◆ America Online: **keyword: newsgroups**

42. To configure the Netscape Collabra:

- In **Netscape Communicator**, open **Netscape Collabra**. This is the newsreader client that comes as part of the Communicator suite.

    √ *The terms Discussion Groups and News Groups are frequently used interchangeably.*

    ◆ Open the **Netscape Collabra** program by clicking the Collabra icon on the Communicator component toolbar

    (*see page 4*) or click **Start**, **Programs**, **Netscape Communicator**, **Netscape Collabra**.

        √ *The Netscape Message Center window will display. The Collabra and the e-mail Message Center interfaces work together.*

    ◆ Select **Edit**, **Preferences**.

    ◆ Click the (**+**) sign next to the Mail & Groups heading to display the sub-headings. Click on the **Groups Server** option.

    ◆ Enter the **Discussion groups (news) server** information you got from your ISP or network systems administrator.

        √ *It is recommended that you don't change any of the default settings at this time.*

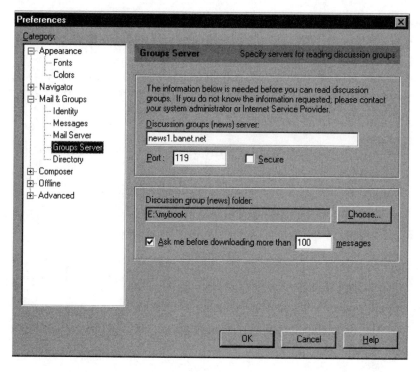

√ *The only default setting you may want to change is the Discussion groups folder. If you want to choose a different folder to save your newsgroup mail, click the **Choose** button and select a different folder (see Windows 95: Just the Basics) or create a new folder.*

♦ Click on the **Messages** option from the Mail & Groups options list.

♦ Select the **Groups** mail options you desire.

♦ Click **OK**.

42a. To access Discussion (News) groups from your news server using Collabra:

- Double-click the news server from the Netscape Collabra main screen, the Netscape Message Center.

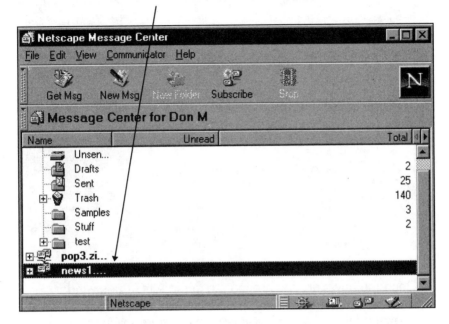

- Click **File, Subscribe to Discussion Groups**.

  √ *The Subscribe to Newsgroups screen opens.*

- Collabra will begin to search your ISP news server for a list of newsgroups. Depending on the traffic to your ISP and the speed of your computer and modem, it may take a while to load the newsgroups into the **All Groups** list box.

  √ *Make sure the **All Groups** tab is selected.*

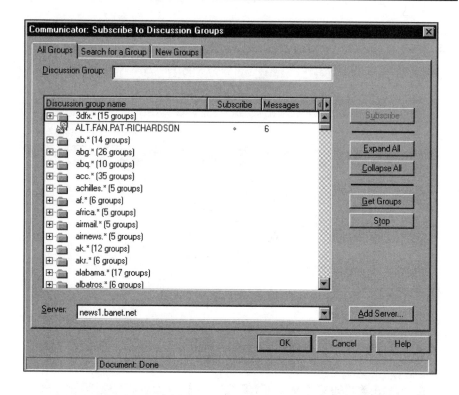

- Once the news groups are loaded in the All Groups window, click on the (+) sign next to each main Discussion group folder to expand the folder and display the newsgroups in that folder. The (-) sign collapses the main folder and hides the Discussion groups.

    OR

    - Click **Expand All** to open all Discussion group main folders.

    - Click **Collapse All** to hide all Discussion groups.

43. To subscribe to a Discussion group:

- Select the newsgroup and click the **Su̱bscribe** button.

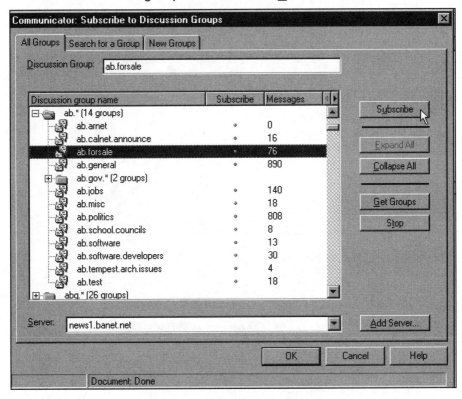

- Collabra will automatically enter your request and a ✔ will appear in the subscribe column of the Discussion group name window to confirm your subscription.

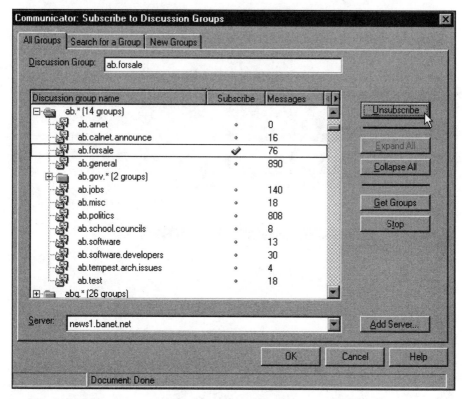

To unsubscribe to a Discussion group from the Discussion group window:

- Select the Discussion group.
- Click the **Unsubscribe** button.

43a. To read messages contained in the newsgroups you've subscribed to:

- It is a good idea to begin your Usenet experience by typing the newsgroup **news.newusers.questions** and subscribing to it. This newsgroup lists articles on the rules and regulations of Usenet.

  ♦ From the Netscape Message Center screen click on (**+**) sign next to your news server to expand the folder and display the Discussion (News) groups to which you've subscribed.

    √ *To collapse the folder list, click the (-) sign next to the main folder.*

  ♦ Double-click on the desired group from the list.

    √ *The discussion group opens in its own window.*

  ♦ Click on the message from the message list. You can now view it in the preview pane or double-click on the message to open the message in its own window. *See pages 14-16 for more information on message window features.*

  ♦ If you open a message in its own window, click the [image] in the upper right-hand corner of the title bar to return to the Message list.

  OR

  Click **File**, **Close** to close the current message window.

  OR

  Click the Collabra icon on the taskbar to return to the main Collabra page.

  OR

  Click **File**, **Exit** to close Collabra.

44. To search for a specific newsgroup using Netscape Collabra:

♦ Click **File**, **Subscribe** to Discussion Groups,

♦ Click the **Search for a Group** tab.

♦ Enter the group name in the **Search for** box.

♦ Click the **Search Now** button.

OR

Press **Enter**.

• To subscribe to a discussion group from your search results, click the **Subscribe** button.

45. To configure Outlook Express for Newsgroups:

• Open **Outlook Express** from the Explorer components toolbar or click **Start** , **Internet Explorer**, **Outlook Express**.

• Click **Tools**, **Accounts**.

• Click **Add**, **News**.

√ *Enter the information asked for by the **Internet Connection Wizard**. You will need your news server address. Contact your ISP for this information. This section assumes you have already configured Outlook to accept e-mail.*

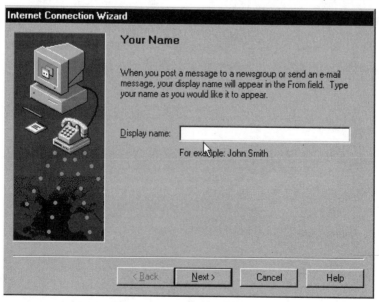

- Type the name you would like to appear on a newsgroup list when you post a message and click **Next**.

- Enter your complete e-mail address in the **E-Mail address** field and then click **Next**.

- Type the news server information you received from your ISP or systems administrator in the **News (NNTP) server** field and click **Next**.

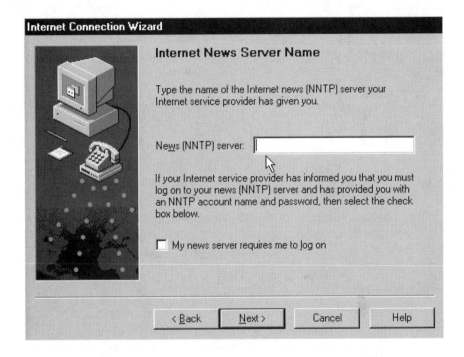

√ *You probably will not be required to log in to the news server you use, but you should check with your ISP to verify this information. If you find that you do have to log in to access the news server, check the **My news server requires me to log on** box and enter your login name and password on the screen that follows.*

- Type a name to use for your News connection in the **Internet news account name** field and click **Next**.

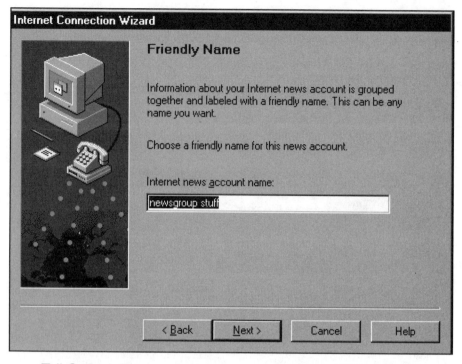

Internet Connection Wizard

Friendly Name

Information about your Internet news account is grouped together and labeled with a friendly name. This can be any name you want.

Choose a friendly name for this news account.

Internet news account name:

newsgroup stuff

| < Back | Next > | Cancel | Help |

- Tell Outlook Express how you connect to your ISPs news server. If you choose the phone line option, click **Next**.

  √ *If you've chosen one of the other two options, click Next to end the configuration setup.*

- Choose your modem from the pull-down menu and click **Next**.

- Select your dial-up connection from the list provided.

  √ *You probably have connected to the Internet before in which case you can check the Dial-Up connection option **Use an Existing Dial-Up Connection** and then select your ISP from the list. If not, you will have to set a Dial-Up Connection.*

- Click **Finish** to complete the configuration.

  √ *You can click the **Back** button to return to any of the previous screens and change information. Click the **Next** button to return to this final screen.*

46. To access newsgroups from your news server using Outlook Express:

- Open Outlook Express, click on your news server from the Outlook screen. The news server is listed as whatever you named it during set-up.

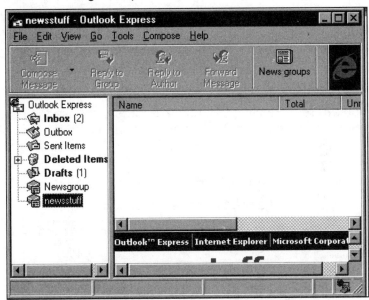

- When prompted to list available newsgroups, click **OK**. Outlook Express will download the list of newsgroups available to you from your news server.

- The list of newsgroups will load into the window.

46a. The first time you connect to your news server, you will have to download the list of newsgroups available to you:

- If you are continuing from the configuration process, you may receive a prompt asking you to view a list of available newsgroups. Click **Yes**. You will see this prompt each time you connect to your new server until you subscribe to at least one newsgroup.

  OR

  If you are reconnecting to Outlook Express, choose the news server you added from the Outlook folders on the left side of

  the main screen and click [News groups] on the toolbar.

- If prompted to list available newsgroups, click **Yes**.

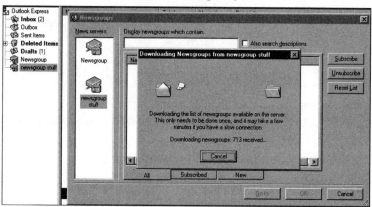

√ *When you to connect to your news server for the first time, Outlook Express will download the list of newsgroups available to you.*

- The list of newsgroups will load into the News groups window.

47. To search newsgroups with Outlook:

- It will be very difficult to look at every newsgroup listed to find one you like. The best way to find a newsgroup that you may be interested in is to do a newsgroup search.

- Enter the keywords of your interest as you would any search, in the **Display newsgroups which contain** box.

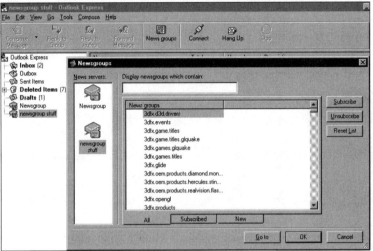

√ *You should see a window similar to the one above once all the newsgroups have been loaded. This is a list of all the newsgroups available to you through your ISP new server.*

- If the above window is not the one displayed, click **Tools**, **Newsgroups**.

OR

Click on the toolbar.

√ *The Newsgroups box opens.*

- Enter a topic that interests you in the **Display newsgroups which contain** box.

- Outlook will search automatically. Do not press Enter. Search results will display automatically.

47a. To subscribe to a newsgroup from the search results window:

- After you subscribe to a newsgroup, articles in that newsgroup will download each time you connect to your news server.

  ◆ Launch Outlook Express and select your news server from the folder list.

  ◆ Click **Tools**, **Newsgroups**.

  ◆ Select a newsgroup from the Newsgroups window and click the **Subscribe** button. You can subscribe to as many newsgroups as you wish.

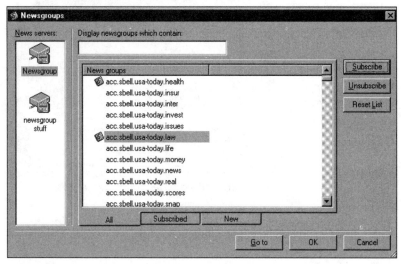

√ *A newspaper icon appears in front of each newsgroup to which you've subscribed.*

  ◆ Click the **Subscribed** tab to see any newsgroups to which you've subscribed.

47b. To read newsgroup articles for newsgroups to which you've subscribed:

- Launch Outlook Express.

- To connect to your news server, click the news server folder from the folder list.

- Click the (+) sign to expand your newsgroup folder. The newsgroups you've subscribed to are listed in the window to the right of the folders list.

- Double-click on a newsgroup. The subject headers for each message will display in this window.

- Select a message to view its contents in the preview pane below the message subject header list.

√ *The preview window allows you to preview the selected message without opening it in its own window.*

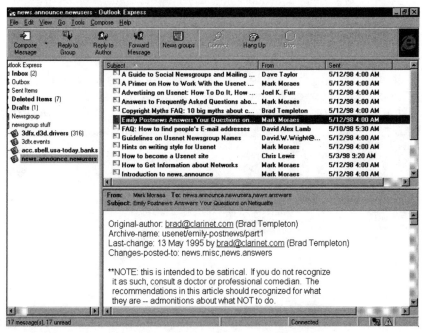

- To open a message in its own window, double-click on the message from the list.

  ◆ If a message is a reply, >> marks appear in front of the text of the original message.

♦ Messages with responses are called a "thread." Follow a message thread to read the original message and all the responses.

♦ Click the **(+)** signs next to the message to read the thread. Responses may also have a thread or a response to the response. Click on the **(+)** sign next to the response to read the response thread.

To read messages to newsgroups to which you haven't subscribed:

♦ Launch Outlook Express.

♦ Click your news server folder.

♦ Click **Tools**, **Newsgroups**

♦ Select a newsgroup.

√ *The newsgroup will be added temporarily to the list of newsgroups in your new server folder.*

• Click the **Go to** button on the Newsgroups main screen (Outlook Express screen).

√ *A list of the subject headers of the selected newsgroup articles will display in the preview pane (see pages 49-50 for more information about the Outlook message screen).*

• Click on the subject heading to display the message in the message preview pane.

• If after reading the articles in the newsgroup you choose to subscribe, right-click on the group name from the folder list box to the left side of the screen and click **Subscribe to this newsgroup**.

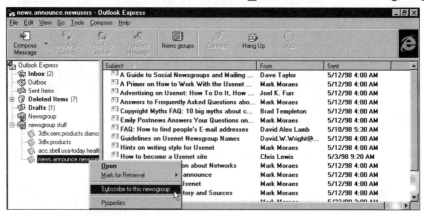

• Click ![News groups] on the toolbar to go back to your list of newsgroups and continue searching.

OR

Exit Outlook Express (File, Exit).

- Click on the Help menu from Outlook Express to get information about reading messages offline, responding to a message and posting a message to a newsgroup.

48. To configure America Online:

- America Online is already configured to access newsgroups from Usenet.

- Click KEYWORD.

- Enter the keyword: **newsgroups** to access the Newsgroups area.

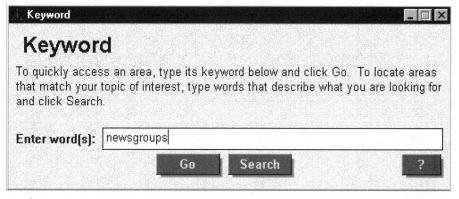

√ AOL asks that you set any mail filter preferences before you go to Usenet.

- Start by clicking Read My Newsgroups from the Usenet/Newsgroups main screen. *See #49 for how to subscribe to a newsgroup.*

  √ *The Newsgroup window will display the article subjects.*

- Double-click on one of the newsgroups to see a list of subjects.

◆ Double-click on a subject from the list to read it.

   √ *A list of message subject headers will display along with the number of messages under each header. A message and the responses to that message is called a "thread."*

◆ If there is more than one article, click to view the next article in the thread.

◆ Click **Sign Off** from the menu bar to exit AOL.

   OR

   Close all newsgroup windows to return to the AOL main screen.

 # 49. To subscribe to a newsgroup in AOL:

• Connect to newsgroups by keyword: **usenet** or **newsgroups**.

• Click **Add Newsgroups** from the Newsgroups main screen.

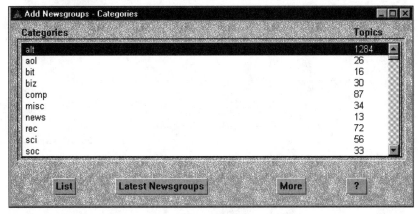

   √ *The Add Newsgroups–Categories screen will display.*

• Double-click on a category *(see #53)* to display a list of topics covered under this hierarchy.

   √ *A new window will display a list of topics for the hierarchy you've selected.*

- Double-click a topic to display the list of newsgroups.
- Select a newsgroup that interests you from the list.

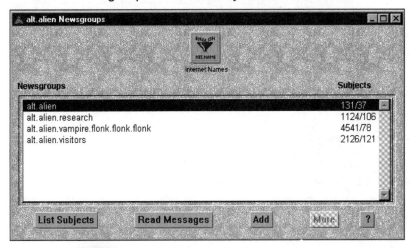

- Click the **Add** to subscribe.

    √ *The newsgroup will be added to your personal newsgroup list. To see this list, click the Read my newsgroups icon on the Internet Newsgroups/Usenet screen.*

    √ *To read articles from newsgroups to which you've subscribed, click on the Read my newsgroups icon.*

- If desired, exit AOL.

50. To read newsgroup articles by subject:

- Follow steps 1-5 under *#49*.

- Click │ List Subjects │ to display the subjects of each article posted.

  √ *A list of article subject headers will display along with the number of articles under each header. This number is also called the "thread." When you read the thread, you are reading each article listed under the selected subject.*

- Select a subject and click │ Read Messages │ to display the article(s).

- Click │ Subject –>> │ to read the article(s) under the next subject.

  OR

  Click │ Message –> │ to read the next message in the thread.

  √ *The **Message** button will only be available if there is more than one message in the thread.*

- Close AOL or close the newsgroup windows and continue on to something else.

51. To search newsgroups in AOL:

- Click Search All Newsgroups from the Newsgroup/Usenet main screen.

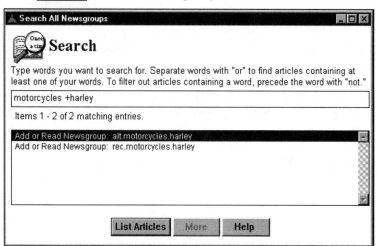

  √ *Search the database following the search instructions above the keyword box.*

- Type in the keywords of your search.

- Click **List Articles**.

  OR

  Press **Enter**.

  √ Click the **More** button for more entries. The **More** button will only be available if there are more newsgroups available.

- Double-click a newsgroup that interests you from the list displayed.

- Click the <u>Subscribe to newsgroup</u> link.

  √ The newsgroup will be added to your personal newsgroup list. To see this list, click the Read my newsgroups icon on the Internet Newsgroups/Usenet screen.

  OR

  Click <u>List articles in newsgroup</u>.

  √ A list of article subject headers will display along with the number of articles under each header. This number is also called the "thread." When you read the thread, you are reading each article listed under the selected subject.

- Select a subject from the list displayed.

- To display the article(s) under the selected subject, click **Read**.

  OR

  Double-click on the article.

- If there is more than one article, click **Message ->** to view the next article in the thread.

  OR

  If you would like to go to the next subject and read the message(s), click **Subject ->>**.

- Click **Sign Off** from the menu bar to exit AOL.

  OR

  Close all newsgroup windows to return to the AOL main screen.

- To learn more about how to work with Newsgroups, go back to the Internet Newsgroups/Usenet main screen and click on the How To... or the FAQs, Tips, & Troubleshooting links.

52. Before you start exploring Usenet, it is important to know the rules and regulations.

- There are no federal laws regulating Usenet and no one actually polices newsgroups. However, newsgroups participants fiercely watch over their own newsgroups.

- It is recommended that you go to *news.announce.newusers* to become familiar with the rules and regulations of Usenet.

- You are now a "newbie" which means you are new to the world of Usenet and there are a few things you need to know about the do's and don'ts of using Usenet. You will be reprimanded by members of the Usenet community for your ignorance or defiance. *See #56.*

- You can also go to the help menu on the Netscape, Outlook Express, or America Online to get more information on Usenet and newsgroups.

53. The addresses look different than the addresses I see for Web sites. What do they mean?

- When you type a newsgroup address, no protocol (*http* or *ftp*) is needed. Simply type the address as it appears.

Newsgroups are organized by hierarchy:

- Under the main hierarchy are sub-headings which are also called hierarchies. The seven most popular hierarchies are:

  - **news**
    news about Usenet newsgroups, not current events

  - **rec**
    includes recreational topics such as movies, sports and automobiles

  - **soc**
    social issues, including many newsgroups dedicated to specific world cultures

  - **talk**
    opinions

- ◆ **compu**
  computer-related issues, operating systems, networking
- ◆ **misc**
  taxes, kids
- ◆ **sci**
  physics, astronomy, and biology
- All newsgroup addresses begin with the main hierarchy, followed by the subject hierarchy's information:
  - ◆ For example: *Soc.culture.costa-ric*
  - ◆ The address indicates that this newsgroup deals with social issues in Costa Rica's culture.

54. How do I search for articles on Usenet?

- One of the best ways to find past articles on Usenet is to go to the dejanews search site:

  ## http://www.dejanews.com

- You can search by archive category, subject category, keyword matches, group, author, or subject.

- This site has the most comprehensive catalog of past Usenet articles on the Web. Search this site as you would any other. Use the common search tips found in the *Web Searches: The Needle in the Haystack* section of this book.

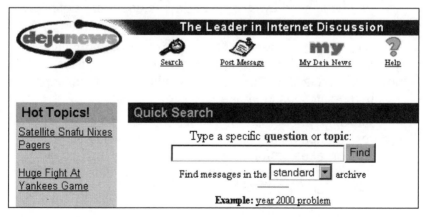

55. Can you post anything on a newsgroup? How is it monitored?

- You can post an opinion, share information, or reply to a query by posting an article to the newsgroup. Anything can be posted as long as it is relevant to the newsgroup and appropriate for the audience. *See #56 for tips on what not to post.*

- You can also post binary files to a newsgroup. Binary files are formatted data which includes multimedia files.

- A newsgroup listing with "binaries" as one of the hierarchies contains articles that are binary files.

- Although files are not necessarily censored, they don't generally stay on your host computer (ISP news server) for over two weeks. There would not be enough room on the Usenet system or your new server to keep all the millions of articles posted. Generally after a article has been on the server for two weeks, it is deleted.

- Keeping up with new articles on Usenet requires your constant attention to what's being posted on the newsgroup to which you subscribe.

56. Are there any specific netiquette guidelines for posting a message?

- Yes. Since, theoretically, something that you post at a Usenet site may be viewed by millions of people, there are definitely some things to keep in mind before you post something.

- Most Usenet sites have a FAQ (frequently asked question) section that pertains to that group. When you visit a new newsgroup, this is the first place you should go. Questions include specific posting rules.

- Read through past entries to get a sense of the group. Different groups on the same topic may have very different attitudes or takes on topic. This will help you keep in sync with the other members. Or, you may find that this is not the newsgroup for you.

- Stick to the subject.

- Be sure that your message will not be misunderstood. If you are at all worried that it may be misinterpreted, add a few emoticons to show that you are only joking.

- Try to keep messages to a manageable length.

- Chain letters or pyramid schemes are illegal. Never post one at a newsgroup or anywhere else on the Internet. Also, never post any type of solicitation for commercial products.

- Avoid cross-posting messages. This is when you post the same message to several newsgroups. When you cross-post a message, chances are the message won't be appropriate for all the groups that will view your message. Keep your messages group-specific.

Viruses: Computer Bugs

Viruses are malicious programs designed to cause deliberate destruction to someone's computer. They are instructions or code that reproduce as they attach themselves to other programs without the user's knowledge.

Viruses can be programmed to do anything a computer can do. Viruses are a nuisance, but if you take the necessary precautions to deal with them, they are manageable. To combat viruses, you must understand the nature of these programs, how they work, and how they can be disinfected.

Viruses are potentially destructive to one file or to an entire hard disk, whether the file or hard disk is one used in a standalone computer or in a multi-user network. Viruses come in many different forms; some are more debilitating than others. Like biological viruses, computer viruses need a host, or a program, to infect. Once infection has been transferred, the viruses can spread like wildfire through the entire library of files.

 57. I somehow got a computer virus. I have no idea where I got it or how. Any thoughts?

- They can come from a couple of places:
    - ◆ an infected diskette
    - ◆ downloading an infected file from a bulletin board, the Internet, or an online service
- Knowing how viruses are transmitted will make you sensitive to the possibility of getting one. Read on.

58. What types of viruses are there?

- Viruses come in two categories:
  - ◆ boot sector viruses
  - ◆ file viruses
- **Boot sector** viruses may also be called system sector viruses because they attack the system sector. System or boot sectors contain programs that are executed when the PC is booted. System or boot sectors do not have files. The hardware reads information in the area in the bootup sections of the computer. Because these sectors are vital for PC operation, they are prime target areas for viruses.
- Two types of system sectors exist: DOS sectors and partition sectors. PCs characteristically have a DOS sector and one or more sectors created by the partitioning command, FDISK, or proprietary partitioning software. Partition sectors are commonly called Master Boot Records (MBR). Viruses that attach to these areas cause serious damage.
- **File viruses** are more common. Characteristically, a file virus infects by overwriting part or all of a file. Or, as in the case of the widespread concept virus, a virus can change the format of a file. The concept virus changed all application files into template files.

 ## 59. I've heard about viruses that lurk inside your computer and then attack one day. Is that true?

- Viruses come in many sizes and with various symptoms. For example, a virus may attach itself to a program immediately and begin to infect an entire hard disk. Or, the virus can be written to attack at a specific time according to your computer clock. For example, the Michelangelo virus strikes on his birthday each May.
- Some viruses are written so that they delay letting you know of their existence until they have done major damage.

60. How can I tell if I have a virus?
Will my computer just stop working?

- Hopefully, you will install antivirus software in your PC that will identify viruses and make you immediately aware that you have a viral intruder. Otherwise, you may experience different symptoms such as:
  - slow processing
  - animation or sound appearing out of nowhere
  - unusually heavy disk activity
  - odd changes in files
  - unusual printer activity

61. What can I do to prevent viruses?

- Most viruses spread when you boot your computer from an infected diskette. As a healthy precaution, boot only from the hard drive.
  - Backup all files.
  - Even new software can come with a virus; scan every diskette before use.
  - Mark all software program attributes as read-only.
  - Research and update antivirus products on an ongoing basis to have the latest protection.
  - Since there are many types of viruses, one type of antivirus protection won't disinfect all viruses. The safest approach is to install a multiple antivirus program library.

62. Which antivirus program should I get?

- There are several highly recommended antivirus programs. Among them are:

Dr. Solomon's Anti-Virus Deluxe
http://www.drsolomon.com/

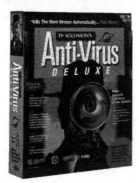

♦ Dr. Solomon's Anti-Virus program uses NetGuard Internet Scanning technology to detect and destroy viruses. It also includes exclusive WinGuard scanner and SOS™ disk to provide the best virus protection from Internet downloads, shared files, and e-mail.

Norton AntiVirus 4.0 for Windows 95 and Windows NT
http://www.symantec.com/us.index.html

♦ One of the most popular antivirus programs, Norton AntiVirus (NAV) 4.0 for Windows 95/NT protects against all possible sources of infection, including the Internet, floppy disks, e-mail attachments, shared files, and networks. You can keep Norton AntiVirus up-to-date by downloading new virus definitions created by the Symantec AntiVirus Research Center (SARC).

♦ Visit *Symantec.com* for the latest information on antivirus research and software.

Netiquette: Rules of the Road

Netiquette is the art of civilized communications among people on the Internet. There are certain Net manners that everyone should use when sending e-mail messages, chat room messages, or newsgroup messages. Follow these guidelines.

63. When sending e-mail, always include a message header.

- Always include a subject in the message heading. This makes it easy for the recipient to organize messages in folders by topic and to find a message by browsing through message headers. It also gives the recipient an idea of why you're writing.

64. Keep your voice down.

- Do not use capital letters. To the recipient, it feels like YOU ARE SHOUTING, and shouting is rude. Instead, enclose text that you want to emphasize with asterisks. For example: *I wanted *veggie* burgers. You know I don't eat *meat*.*

65. Be careful with the tone you use.

- E-mail does not afford you the luxury of nuance. With the absence of inflection, the recipient can easily misinterpret your message. Use emoticons to establish your intent. They may seem silly but they help clarify your intentions. A smiley emoticon tells the recipient that you are really joking. Use sparingly. If, indeed, you're not joking, you're flaming. *See #72 and #73.*

66. Don't flame!

- Do not send flame messages. These are obnoxious, offensive, or otherwise disturbing messages. If you send this type of message to a newsgroup, 30,000 people who read your flame will think less of you. The fact that they don't know you is no excuse. If you receive flame mail, press the Delete button rather than the Reply button.

67. Once a message leaves your computer it can be available to anyone with an e-mail address or access to a computer.

- Messages sent over the Internet are not private. Your message is in writing and nothing can prevent someone from forwarding it to anyone they please. Assume that anyone with access to a computer and an e-mail address has the potential to read your message.

68. If your message is long or if the e-mail attachment you send will take some time to download let the recipient know.

- If you send a long message, it is a good idea to tell the recipient in the subject header. If you decide to send an e-mail attachment that requires a long time to download, let the recipient know so that they can decide whether to download it or read it later.

69. Check your spelling.

- Avoid sending messages with spelling errors by spell checking your messages before you send them. There is a spell check feature in Netscape, Internet Explorer, and America Online 4.0. Several e-mail programs also include a spell check feature. Or, you can compose your e-mail in a word processing program, spell check it there, and copy and paste it into an e-mail message. *See Windows 95: Just the Basics.*

70. Chain letters are considered spam.

- Never initiate or forward a chain letter. Some service providers will cancel your membership if you do so, as they are trying to protect their members from unwanted mail. Most people wouldn't send a chain letter to twenty people via snail mail, so don't abuse the e-mail system by doing it electronically. *See Spam: The New Junk Mail.*

71. Here is a very comprehensive site dedicated to helping you brush up on your Net manners:.

Netiquette Home Page

The Netiquette Home Page

http://www.albion.com/netiquette/index.html

- This page lists hyperlinks to pages on Netiquette contributed by Internet users. You will find interesting, amusing, and very important material in these pages.

 72. What are emoticons?

- Since you cannot see the people with whom you communicate on the Internet, emoticons are symbols you can use to convey emotion in your messages. Be sure to use these cute symbols *only* in your personal communications.

 73. Common Emoticons:

- Use these symbols to convey emotions in your messages. To see the faces in these symbols, turn the page to the right.

>:->	Angry	:-(	Sad
5:-)	Elvis	:-@	Scream
:-)	Happy	:-#	Secret (lips are sealed)
()	Hug	:P	Sticking Tongue Out
:-D	Joking	:-O	Surprised
:*	Kiss	:-J	Tongue in Cheek
:/)	Not Funny	;-)	Wink

74. Frequently Used Acronyms:

- On the next page, you'll find some acronyms that you will encounter in Internet messages (such as e-mail, newsgroup messages, and chat room discussions).

- Be sure to check online to see what's new.

- For more emoticons and acronyms, go to the Emoticons & Smileys page:

http://home.earthlink.net/~gripweeds/emoticon.htm

ADN	Any day now
ASAP	As soon as possible
B4N	Bye for now
BRB	Be right back
BTW	By the way
F2F	Face to face
FAQ	Frequently asked questions
FWIW	For what it's worth
FYI	For your information
GMTA	Great minds think alike
IMO	In my opinion
IRL	In real life
JIC	Just in case
KWIM	Know what I mean
LOL	Laugh out loud
OTOH	On the other hand
RTM	Read the manual
TIA	Thanks in advance
TMOT	Trust me on this
TTYTT	To tell you the truth
WFM	Works for me

Compressed Files: Zip It!

There are times when you may need to send multiple files to someone and your mail server does not support multiple file attachments. So what do you do? Send ten e-mails, each with a separate attachment? Other times you may have only one file to send, but it's a large file that would take forever to upload (send) and for the recipient to download (receive). For times like these, you need to use a program like WinZip, which can compress several files or one file into an archive.

The WinZip program is easy to use. Once installed it will attach itself to your Windows program, and, in most cases, will open automatically when you download files that need unzipping. If you use AOL, you can also use WinZip to open e-mail attachments or downloads that AOL says are too large for the program to open. *See #14.*

The following information deals with WinZip and zipping and unzipping files. For information on attaching files and e-mailing them, see the Netscape Messenger, Outlook Express, or American Online E-mail sections in the Basics section of this book.

 75. **What does zipping a file mean?**

- It means that you are creating an archive of one or more files and compressing those files into a fraction of their original size.

- Zipped files take up less computer space and can be sent electronically very quickly.

- Any file type or any combination of files can be zipped and stored in one archive. Remember that the recipient of your archive must have the necessary applications in order to view the files.

76. How do I get the WinZip program?

- WinZip is available from most of the popular shareware sites on the Web. Try *http://www.tucows.com*. Once you've connected to the site and gone through the links to connect to a server near you, click on the link to the Windows 95/98 area.

- Once there go to the General Tools category and click on the link to Compression Utilities. Scroll down to find WinZip and click the download button to work with a trial version of the software. It's free to try and $29.00 to keep.

- You can also buy this program at almost any store that sells software.

 ## 77. How do I install WinZip?

- To install WinZip, double-click on the *winzip95.exe* icon. A WinZip wizard will walk you through the setup.

- It is recommended that you choose the WinZip Classic, not Wizard, in the setup dialog box. The following procedures only deal with Classic WinZip.

 ## 78. How do I zip a file(s) using WinZip?

- You must first create an archive or a shell in which the files you want to zip are going to be housed. This is the only way you will be able to combine several files under one name. Don't be discouraged by the number of steps you see below. It really is very simple and goes very quickly.

- Here's the procedure:

    ◆ Open the WinZip program from your desktop or from **Start**, **Programs**, **WinZip**.

    ◆ Click the **New** archive button on the WinZip toolbar.
      √ *The new archive dialog box will display.*

♦ Choose the drive and folder from the **Create In** box where you want the zip archive to be stored.

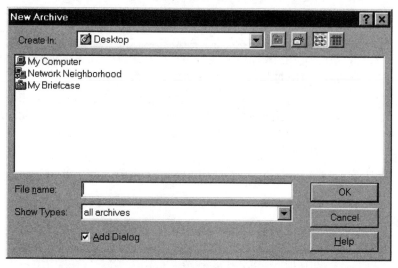

♦ Type a name of your choosing for the archive in the **File name** box. Do not enter the names of the files being compressed.

√ *The name you choose for the archive must be unique. It can not be the name of a zip archive already existing in the drive and folder you chose.*

√ *If you are adding two or more files, make sure the **Add Dialog** box is checked. This will enable you to add multiple files easily.*

♦ Click **OK**.

♦ Once the Add screen displays, choose the location of the file or files you want to add to the archive from the **Add from** drop-down list.

♦ Click on the first file.

OR

If there is more than one file and the files are in consecutive order, click on the first file, hold down the Shift key and click on the last file you want to add to the archive. Release the Shift key. All the consecutive files are highlighted and are now displayed in the **File name** box.

OR

If the files are not consecutive, select the first file and hold down the Ctrl key. Click on each file you want to include in the archive. The non-consecutive files will be highlighted. Release the Ctrl key.

- Click the **Add** button.
  - √ *WinZip will compress the file or files and add them to the now displayed archive file list window.*

  - √ *If you are adding each file to the archive individually, click the* *button from the archive file list screen and repeat steps 6-8 until the archive is complete.*

- Click **File**, **Exit** to close WinZip.
  - √ *The zip file is automatically saved to the location you specified in step 3.*

79. How do I open a zip file archive?

- Zip files are identified in your file list by a [icon] before the file name and a *.zip* extension. Once you have installed WinZip, any zip file you download or receive via e-mail (except AOL which has its own zip utility) should automatically launch the WinZip program. The WinZip main screen will list all the files in the archive.

- If WinZip does not launch automatically or if you want to open a zip file from a disk or another source:

  - Launch WinZip by double-clicking on the WinZip application icon.

  - Click [Open] from the toolbar.

  - From the Open Archive screen choose the location of the zip archive from the **Look in** box.

  - Double-click on the file from the file list.
    - √ *The WinZip main window will display the contents of the archive.*

  - Double-click on each file that you wish to decompress and open.
    - √ *WinZip launches the necessary application and the file opens within that application. If you don't have the correct application installed on your computer, the files can not be viewed.*

80. Once I view a file, how can I save it outside of the archive?

- Once the file is open you can click **File**, **Save As** from the application that opened the decompressed file. The file will be saved in its decompressed state.

- You can save a file from the WinZip main window by:

  - Selecting the file(s) from the list. *See #78 for information on selecting multiple files.*

  - Clicking from the toolbar.

  - When the Extract dialog box displays, choose the drive and folder where you want to save the file(s).

    √ *You can also create a new folder to store the extracted file by clicking the **New Folder** button.*

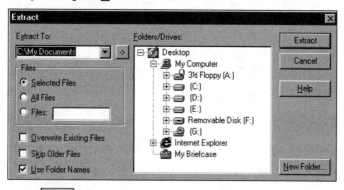

  - Click . The file(s) will be copied in its decompressed state to the new location.

    √ *A zip archive and all the zipped files it contains remain in the saved to location until it is deleted.*

81. How do I delete a file from the archive?

- If the archive is open, select the file and press the **Delete** key.
  OR

  Click **Actions** from the WinZip menu and select **Delete**.

82. Are there any help features in case I get stuck?

- The Help menu is an invaluable resource for answering questions about how to use WinZip. When you first install WinZip, you should read the WinZip tutorial.

- To access the tutorial, launch WinZip, then click Help and select Brief Tutorial. Read through the tutorial so that you will have a clear understanding of how the program works and the zip options that are available. The Hints and Tips sections on the Help menu is another worthwhile resource.

Shareware and Freeware: The Essential Downloads

Log on to the following URLs to download Web and multimedia software, much of which is available free of charge or as shareware, which requires a minimal registration fee.

 ## 83. The Browsers:

Internet Explorer

http://www.microsoft.com/ie/download/

- Internet Explorer 4.0 is the latest version of Microsoft's Internet browser software. It has attracted a lot of attention for both its powerful new features and its role in the Department of Justice investigation of Microsoft for antitrust violations.

- Explorer 4.0's active desktop features allow the browser software to be much more integrated into the Windows operating system you use to run your computer.

- You can also receive active content from the Web using Explorer's "push" technology. Active content lets you choose from among several Web content "channels" to receive automatic information updates to your desktop.

- Other Explorer 4.0 tools include NetMeeting virtual conferencing software and FrontPage Express. NetMeeting helps facilitate virtual meetings held via the Internet and one-to-one telephone calls from your computer. FrontPage Express enables you to create and post your own Web pages.

- Whatever the outcome of the legal wrangling, Explorer is rapidly gaining market acceptance as the leading Web browser. Get your copy free of charge at this site.

Netscape Navigator

http://home.netscape.com/download/index.html

- Netscape Navigator 4.0 is the other major Web browser on the market today and the direct descendant of the Mosaic browser that first swept many users into the world of surfing the Web.

- Netscape Communicator includes Navigator 4.0 and a complete suite of Internet tools, including Messenger for e-mail, Collabra for newsgroups, and Composer for creating Web pages.

- You can also download a complete installation of Netscape Communicator which includes Netscape Netcaster for receiving active channel content, Netscape Conference for online collaboration and the capability to handle rich multimedia content as well as bitstream fonts.

- Though you must pay for Netscape products available at this download site, you can download evaluation versions of new software free of charge. Educational institutions and nonprofit organizations can download a number of Netscape products at no charge.

 ## 84. The Shareware and Freeware Sites:

TUCOWS

http://www.tucows.com

- TUCOWS stands for The Ultimate Collection Of Winsock Software. The site bills itself as the world's best collection of Internet software.

- After logging on to the TUCOWS home page, click the appropriate link for your geographical location (such as United States, Europe, Canada), then click the appropriate state (or other area) link. These geographical links are used to produce faster and more reliable software downloads.

- Next click the appropriate link for your computer's operating system. You will see a directory page listing links for more than 60 different types of Internet software.

- Click on a category link to see a listing of software available in that category for downloading. Listings include a complete description of the software, its hardware requirements, and a rating of the software (by number of cows). Click the Download button next to a particular listing to start downloading.

- Most software available at TUCOWS is either shareware or freeware, though some products offered are only demo versions that may have limited features or time restraints.

Shareware.Com
http://www.shareware.com

- Shareware.Com is another great site for downloading software via the Web. The site is a service of the C/Net Web page, noted for its computer and technology news coverage.

- You can browse the site by clicking on the New Arrivals or Most Popular links, or you can simply enter the name of the software you hope to find in the search engine text box.

- Highlights of available shareware are shown on the home page. Click on a link to go to a description of the shareware and a link to the download page.

The Jumbo Download Network
http://www.jumbo.com

- Yet another great software downloading site is The Jumbo Download Network, which lists more than 250,000 shareware programs and links. Available software is conveniently organized by channels, including Business, Desktop, Internet, Utilities, Games, Entertainment, Developer, and Demo City, which offers the latest commercial demos so you can try before you buy.

85. The Essential Plug-Ins and Multimedia Software:

VDOLive Video Player
http://www.vdo.net/download/

- Download VDOnet Corporation's VDOLive Video Player 3.0 free of charge at this site. VDOLive is the top software for broadcasting and receiving video content over the Internet and is used by many major television networks, including CBS News, MTV, and PBS.

- Click on the VDOLive 3.0 link to begin downloading the software. You must register to download, but otherwise the procedure is free and relatively easy. Only the VDOLive Player software is available for free download. VDOLive server software must be purchased.

- You can also download a trial version of VDOPhone, touted as the first full-color video telephone available for either regular telephone lines or the Internet. VDOPhone lets you see and hear anyone over the Internet with no additional phone charges.

- VDOPhone is currently available for Windows 95 users only. The trial version expires after 5 hours of video reception.

Adobe Acrobat Reader

http://www.adobe.com

- Adobe Acrobat Reader lets you view, navigate, and print many document files available on the Web for downloading.

- To download the Acrobat Reader free of charge, click the Free Plug-Ins and Updates link at the Adobe home page. The link takes you to a file library page that displays a list of nearly thirty software products you can download. Links to download sites for each type of software are displayed by operating system.

- Click the Acrobat Reader link for your computer's operating system. The reader is available for Windows, Macintosh, DOS, UNIX, and OS/2. You will go to a page including short description links and download links for the available versions of Acrobat Reader. Click the Download link to register and begin downloading.

- You can also click the Tryout Software link at the Adobe home page to see descriptions of Adobe's latest multimedia and graphics products as well as download links for trial versions.

Shockwave

http://www.macromedia.com/shockwave/download/

- Macromedia Shockwave facilitates smooth viewing of animation --1,0and multimedia over the Internet. Many Web browsers and online services such as Internet Explorer, Netscape Navigator, and AOL include Shockwave with their software.

- If you want to download Shockwave, go to the Shockwave Download Center at the above URL, and click the Get Shockwave link.

Your browser, e-mail, and Internet Service Provider software are all Windows 95 applications. A basic knowledge of Windows 95 functions will help you deal with these applications more efficiently.

CREATE A NEW FOLDER

■ There are many reasons to create a new folder. When using the Internet, the primary reason will most likely be to organize downloaded files.

86. To create a new file from your browser or an application:

• Click File, Save As.

• From the Save in drop-down list, choose the location for the new folder.

• Click 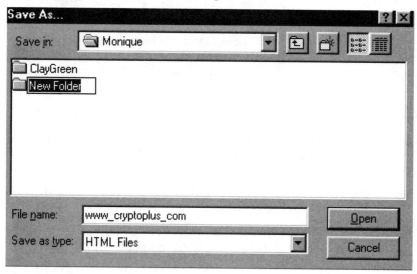 in the Save As dialog box.

Save As...	? X
Save in: 📁 Monique	⬆ 📁 ▦ ▤

📁 ClayGreen
📁 New Folder

File name:	www_cryptoplus_com	Open
Save as type:	HTML Files ▾	Cancel

• Type the new folder name.

• Double-click on the new folder.

√ *The new folder will open in the Save in dialog box.*

- Click the **Save** button to save the file in the new folder.

√ *Your browser should default to this folder each time you save a download.*

OPEN FILES AND FOLDERS

 87. To open files and folders from within any program:

- Click **File**.
- Click **Open**.
- Using the scroll arrow, select the drive from the pull-down menu.
- Double-click on the desired folder.
- Double-click on the desired file.

√ *In both Netscape and Explorer you can open Web pages using similar steps.*

 88. To find files and folders:

- Click **Start** from the taskbar.
- Point to **Find** from the Start menu.
- Click **Files or Folders**.

- Type or select the location to search in the **Look in** box.
- Type or select the file or folder name from the **Named** box.

  OR

  Type key words contained in the document in the **Containing text** box.
- Click **Find Now**.
- Double-click on the file from the file list window to open it.

To stop a search:

- Click **Stop**.

To clear current results:

- Click **New Search**.
- Click **OK**.

FIND FILES AND FOLDERS

- You can search for files that you download or folders that you create by using Windows Explorer. This is a good way to search for files on your computer.

- When Explorer opens, it shows the hierarchy of folders in the All Folders pane on the left and the contents of the selected folder in the Contents pane on the right. *See procedures in this section for help on managing files and folders from Explorer.*

 ## 89. To open Windows Explorer:

√ *You can open Explorer multiple times and drag items between each Explorer window.*

- **Using the Start button:**

  ♦ Click **Start** from the taskbar.

  ♦ Point to **Programs**.

  ♦ Click **Windows Explorer**.

- **By right-clicking:**

  ♦ Right-click the desired drive, folder icon, or the Start button.

    √ *You can also right-click permanent Windows folders like My Computer, Network Neighborhood, and Recycle Bin.*

  ♦ Click **Explorer**.

90. To use Explorer to browse folders and open files:

√ *These steps will work if you do not have the Explorer 4 Active Desktop. To learn more about the Active Desktop, see Basics, Chapter 7.*

√ *The current folder name displays above the Contents pane in the **Go to a different folder box** on the toolbar.*

- **Open any folder:**
    - ◆ Click the folder icon in All Folders pane.

    OR

    - ◆ Double-click the folder icon in the Contents pane.

- **Go to a different folder:**
    - ◆ Show toolbar by going to **View, Toolbar**.
    - ◆ Select desired folder from the Go to a different folder drop-down list.

- **Open parent folder:**
    - ◆ Show toolbar by going to **View, Toolbar**.
    - ◆ Click the **Up One Level** button.

- **Expand folder levels:**
    - ◆ From the All Folders pane, click the ⊞ to the left of any folder to show folder contents.

- **Collapse folder levels:**
    - ◆ From the All Folders pane, click the ⊟ to the left of any folder to hide sub-folders.

- **Open a file:**
    - ◆ Double-click the file icon in the Contents pane to the right of the Folder pane.

MOVE FILES AND FOLDERS

- You can move file folders to a different drive or destination.

 91.To move files:

- **By dragging:**
    - ◆ Make sure that the items to move and the destination are in view.
        - √ *The destination can be a window, icon, or the desktop.*
    - ◆ Select files and/or folders to move. *See #78.*
    - ◆ Drag the selected file over to the destination folder.
        - √ *Windows highlights destination icon or shows selection outline over destination window.*
- **If destination is a folder on another drive:**
    - ◆ Select the file and/or folder to move.
    - ◆ Press and hold the **Shift** key.
    - ◆ Release mouse button and key, if used, to complete the move.
    - √ *When you move an entire folder, the folder is cut from the original location.*
- **Using the menu:**
    - √ *This method is not available from the desktop.*
    - ◆ Open folder containing the items to move.
    - ◆ Select files and folders to move.
    - ◆ Click **Edit, Cut**
        - √ *The cut file appears ghosted.*

To paste on the desktop:
- ◆ Right-click empty area on the desktop.
- ◆ Click **Paste**.

To paste in another folder or drive:
- ◆ Open the destination folder or drive.
- ◆ Click **Edit, Paste**.

92. To select files and folders:

√ *Selects files and folders from the desktop, a folder window, the Explorer Contents pane, and the Find results list.*

- **Select one file or folder:**
    - ◆ Click the file or folder icon.
- **Select multiple files and folders:**
    - ◆ Press **Ctrl** and click each desired file and folder.
- **Select a group of files and folders:**
    - ◆ Point to a blank area near items to select.
    - ◆ Click and drag an outline over the desired files and folders.

    OR

    - ◆ If the files that you want to select are consecutive, select the first file, hold the **Shift** key and click the last file to select simultaneously. All the files between the first and last file will be selected.
- **Select all files and folders:**
    - √ *This option is not available from the desktop.*
    - ◆ Click **Edit, Select All**.

    OR

    - ◆ Press **Ctrl**+**A**.
- **Select, most, but not all, files and folders:**
    - √ *This method is not available from the desktop.*
    - ◆ Press **Ctrl** and click the files and folders you do not want to select.
    - ◆ Click **Edit, Invert Selection**.
- **Deselect files and folders:**
    - ◆ Click any blank area.

DELETE FILES AND FOLDERS

- As you spend more time on the Internet, your library of downloaded files will begin to grow. Due to hard disk space limitations or your desire to get organized, you will eventually need to start deleting files that are no longer important.

93.To delete files and folders:

√ *Unless you configure Windows differently, deleted files are stored in the Recycle Bin until you empty it or until deleted items take up a specified percentage of available hard disk space.*

- Select file or folder to delete. *See #78.*
- Press the **Delete** key.

OR

- Right-click on the file or folder.
- Select **Delete**.

COPY OR CUT INFORMATION FROM ONE FILE AND PASTE INFORMATION TO ANOTHER

- It is easy to cut or copy almost anything from one document to another destination such as an e-mail message or vice versa.

94.To select text in a document:

√ *Selects text prior to applying commands such as Cut and Copy.*

- **To select text:**
  - ◆ Place cursor at the start point of the text you want to select.
  - ◆ Drag mouse holding the left mouse button down as you move through text to select.
    - √ *Windows highlights selected text.*
- **To cancel text selection:**
  - ◆ Click anywhere in the document workspace.

95.To cut or copy text or graphic in document to Clipboard:

√ *Anything placed in Clipboard will stay there until you move something else to the Clipboard.*

- Select the text or graphic to cut or copy.
- Click **Edit**.

OR

- Right-click on the selected text.
- Click **Cut** to move the selection to the clipboard. The selected text or graphic is cut from the screen.

OR

- Click **Copy** to make a copy of the selected text and move it to the Clipboard.

96.To copy screen image to Clipboard:

√ *This procedure will copy the entire computer window—including toobars.*

- Go to screen you wish to capture.
  - ♦ Press ▨.

97.To paste data from Clipboard into document:

√ *Data must be compatible for the application receiving the data.*

- After selecting and copying to the Clipboard, open the application that will receive data.

√ *You can coy text documents into all e-mail programs.*

- **By right-clicking:**
  - ♦ Right-click the workspace where the data will be pasted.
  - ♦ Click **Paste**.
- **Using menu:**
  - ♦ Click the workspace where the data will be pasted.
  - ♦ Click **Edit, Paste**.

WORKING WITH WINDOWS

■ While you are downloading a file you can continue to use your browser by minimizing the download window. You may need to maximize a window in order to access information in another application. Below find information on how to work with windows within Windows 95.

98. To minimize a window:

- **Using the Minimize button:**
  - ◆ Click the window's minimize button in the upper right-hand corner of the window.
- **Using the control symbol:**
  - ◆ Click the window's control symbol in the upper left-hand corner of the application or file window. For example, in Internet Explorer or **Netscape** in Netscape.
  - ◆ Click **Minimize**.
- **Using the taskbar:**
  - ◆ Right-click folder or application button on taskbar.
  - ◆ Click **Minimize**.
- **All windows using taskbar:**
  - ◆ Right-click on any empty area on the taskbar.
  - ◆ Click **Minimize All Windows**.

99. To maximize a window:

- **Using the Maximize button:**
  - ◆ Click the window's maximize button in the upper right-hand corner of the screen.
- **Using the control symbol:**
  - ◆ Click the window's control symbol on the left side of the title bar. For example, in Internet Explorer or **Netscape** in Netscape.
  - ◆ Click **Maximize**.
- **Using the title bar:**
  - ◆ Double-click the window's title bar.

- **Using the taskbar:**
  - ◆ Right-click the folder or application button on the taskbar.
  - ◆ Click **Maximize**.
    OR
    Double-click the folder or application button.

 ## 100. To restore a maximized window:

- **Using the restore button:**

  - ◆ Click the window's restore button .

- **Using the control symbol:**
  - ◆ Click window's control symbol in the upper left-hand corner of the window.
  - ◆ Click **Restore**.
- **Using the title bar:**
  - ◆ Double-click the window's title bar.
- **Using the taskbar:**
  - ◆ Right-click folder or application button on taskbar.
  - ◆ Click **Restore**.

 ## 101. To close a window:

- **Using the close button:**

  - ◆ Click the window's close button ![X].

- **Using the control symbol:**
  - ◆ Click the window's control symbol in the upper left corner of the window.
  - ◆ Click **Close**.
- **Using the keyboard:**
  - ◆ Press **Alt + F4**.

  √ *This will close the entire application. Do not use this procedure to close single windows within an application.*

- **Using the taskbar:**
  - ◆ Right-click folder or application button on taskbar.
  - ◆ Click **Close**.

Index

Index